Life on a Gelato Diet

Everyday expeditions with an
American in Bolzano, Italy

L. Lee McIntyre

Life on a Gelato Diet

Everyday expeditions with an American in Bolzano, Italy

L. Lee McIntyre

This book is for sale at www.amazon.com

This version was published on 2014-04-17

For my father, who taught me it's the people and their
stories that make places come alive

Contents

CONTENTS

Preface

One day you're fantasizing about moving to Europe, and then suddenly you're living in Bolzano/Bozen, in Northern Italy. You live in a somewhat historic apartment building, built in 1926 by a famous Italian architect whose career was derailed when the Fascists came in and had a preference for boxier architecture. The size of the apartment even approximates your romantic ideal of living in an old Italian palazzo, so it might actually be that Italian fantasy come to life.

Except Bolzano/Bozen is only sort of like living in Italy — it's more like Italy with a twist. It's a town with a subtle blend of Italian style and Tyrolean tradition, nestled at the foot of the beautiful Dolomite Mountains. Fascinating in a way you'd never have dreamed, with a charm all its own.

My story isn't the classic one of an American moving to Italy to restore a farmhouse or seek love and romance. While my husband, Chris, pursued a career opportunity in Bolzano/Bozen, I decided to take a sabbatical from my high-tech career as a software designer and pursue my passion for photography while I tried to master the ins and outs of life in a new language.

In this book, we'll roam around the Bolzano on the "Everyday Expeditions" I undertook for a couple of hours each weekday during the three years I lived in Bolzano. We'll do the shopping and say hi to all the people I came to "sort of know" as part of my daily routine. Along the way, I'll share my discoveries and lessons learned about the language of life in the South Tyrol, as well as how I came to refer to living life there on a "gelato diet".

---

*Note: in the Alto Adige, cities, streets, and other places have names in both German and Italian. In the body of this book, I refer to everything only by its Italian name since Italian is the language I focussed on learning during the time I lived in Italy.

Also, where I mention people in Bolzano by name, the people are real, but their names are not.

Welcome to Bolzano

Thanks for meeting me this morning here in Piazza Walther. I can't think of a better place to introduce you to Bolzano; it's always the starting point for my morning errands.

Piazza Walther is the major square in the city center. We'd caught our first glimpse of the square on the Internet before we moved here, via a webcam tucked under that turret on the building over to our right. Two years ago, when we first arrived in town and walked from our hotel to see Piazza Walther in person, it was slightly different from how it looks today. There was a stage that stayed up all summer long that decorated one corner of the square. It displayed a model of the first cable car in these parts, which was celebrating its 100th birthday at the time. I think they claim it was the first cable car in Europe, actually. The car design was strikingly open on the sides, and there were no seat belts to make sure you stayed strapped in as it ascended the steep slope up to Colle, a town above Bolzano. It must have been quite daring to go for a ride in those early days.

Anyway, even two years ago the square was dominated, as it is today, by the big statue of Walther von der Vogelweide. He was a wandering minstrel and celebrated Middle High German lyric poet from the Middle Ages who may or may not have been born in Bolzano.

By the way, Bolzano is the capital of the South Tyrol,

while Innsbruck, Austria is the capital of the North Tyrol. It was originally all just the Tyrol until after World War I, when Italy annexed the South Tyrol as part of the post-war division of spoils. Walther may have been born somewhere in the Tyrol but it's not clear where. So, now both of the Tyrolean capitals claim him as a native son – there is a statue of Walther in Innsbruck, too, but in that city it's tucked away in a small plaza away from the center of town. Walther definitely has pride of place in Bolzano, which uses him as one of the prominent symbols of the town.

It hasn't always been that way, though. As I mentioned, until 1918, Bolzano was part of the Austro-Hungarian Empire, but was annexed by Italy after the war. In the 1920s, after Mussolini took over, he implemented repressive policies against the German-speaking population, aimed at increasing the Italian presence and culture in the region. Not surprisingly, Walther, a Tyrolean hero, didn't really fit in with that plan, and Walther the statue was banished to a small park near the Talvera River. His plaza, where we're standing right now, ultimately became a parking lot.

However, by the 1960s, the parking lot was finally moved underground, and Walther triumphantly regained his rightful place in a peaceful and automobile-free square.

Today, Walther still gazes out over the visitors to his square, majestically rising above the fray, be the fray tourists, road races, or the occasional festival. As the central square in Bolzano, it's typically is the site of any major events that happen throughout the year.

Not least of those events are the ones that are centered on food,

I might add. Food festivals – now that's a fine concept for a celebration. I must say, I do enjoy the food festivals they have here in Italy. When we lived in California there were "Art and Wine" festivals that had art and wine, but little food. Here, the festivals don't usually have art, but they have wine and lots of food. Good combination.

At the festivals in Piazza Walther, the food hasn't always been outstanding, but it's all been fun to try. Certainly one of the most unusual food festivals took place the first October we lived here, the Zucca Festival.

Zucca supposedly means "pumpkin" in Italian; at least that's how it's most often translated in the dictionaries. But I think it more generally means squash. Now I know that pumpkin and squash are from the same vegetable family. And I know what yellow squash, zucchini, acorn squash, and pumpkins look like. However, I don't think I'd ever seen *giant* green squash that look like mutant zucchinis before: they're green and at least a foot-long on the outside, but orange like a pumpkin on the inside. Bizarre.

During the week of the Zucca Festival, restaurants around town had special zucca recipes on the menu. At one place we ate a special zucca-filled tortelloni pasta that looked like the small tortellini pasta, only four-times the size. Those were quite tasty. Plus we had a bruschetta, a toasted bread appetizer that had a few pieces of orange zucca mixed in with the usual tomatos and basil to combine for a rather colorful topping. Not bad.

To better describe the zucca they serve in the foods, I'd say that it has the consistency of squash and the orange color of a pumpkin. Zucca may or may not always be from a pumpkin, since as I mentioned there are vegetables that look like zucchini on the outside that have orange flesh inside.

At the official food stand at the Zucca Festival, we tried a few more odd items. We started with ravioli with a zucca filling: not bad, but not the best example of this dish we've eaten here in Bolzano. The tortelloni we had at that restaurant in town was similar and much better. Next up was a lasagna dish, with zucca mixed into a béchamel sauce. This was a layered dish with lasagna noodles, but it didn't have any cheesy filling like the lasagna I always made with tomato sauce and ricotta back in the U.S.. The festival version was not an exciting dish, although this probably wasn't the best rendition of it. But I'm not sure it would ever be my favorite with the béchamel sauce on pasta.

One of Chris's colleagues had once commented to me that she's never successfully made lasagna; she said it always comes out all stuck together and dry, with the consistency of a pizza crust. I never found out what recipe she was using, but it did strike me at the time that she wasn't talking about the same kind of lasagna dish that I think of as lasagna. Seeing the festival's example of lasagna, I now can imagine how that dish could go wrong and come out stuck together in one dry slab, like pizza crust. So perhaps this lasagna is actually the "real" Italian version – Chris's colleague is originally from Tuscany.

Anyway, we finished off the festival meal with a dessert sampler platter that included several zucca-themed desserts. First up was a zucca mousse, essentially a squash pudding; it was not particularly sweet and we didn't finish it. I had never heard of a squash mousse before. There may be a reason for that.

Bolzano is known for its apples as well as for the zucca, and the dessert platter had a baked apple with a "zucca butter" which was bland. I don't think we finished that, either. The zucca cake was a cross between zucchini bread and pumpkin pie. Not bad, but perhaps it just seemed better when compared to the other two desserts. The dessert platter was accompanied by a sparkling zucca dessert wine: it was sparkling, it was sweet, and it was orange like the zucca. 'Nuff said, eh?

Actually, it wasn't bad – there weren't pieces of zucca in it, as I'd feared there would be. But it wasn't clear what had caused the drink to turn out bright orange.

A couple of months after the Zucca festival in Bolzano, we wound up having a similar concoction in a restaurant in Austria, which actually did combine Prosecco, the Italian sparkling wine, with cooked pieces of zucca at the bottom of the glass. The zucca had been spiced with cinnamon and clove, but it still had a zucca consistency.

Definitely an acquired taste.

Remember, we sacrifice ourselves at these festivals so you don't have to.

But the biggest festival by far in Piazza Walther is the Christmas Market, which kicks into high gear the last weekend of November. The market consists of several dozen wooden stalls, all constructed just for the market (and then dismantled right afterwards).

There are Christmas markets all over the Alto Adige province in Italy, modeled on the ones that happen in both Austria and Germany. The rest of Italy doesn't typically have Christmas markets like the ones in the South Tyrol. For that reason, apparently, lots of Italian tourists make the trip to Bolzano this time of year just to come to the Christmas market.

A few years ago when we were in Florence at Christmastime, there was a "Heidelberg" Christmas market there. We didn't understand at the time why it said it was a "Heidelberg" market, but I guess looking back now, it was because it was a German-style Christmas market that isn't typical in Italy.

Locally, the quaintest one we've been to in the Alto Adige was in Bressanone, about 30 minutes by train from Bolzano.

We read in the paper that some of the ornaments at the stands in the Bolzano market are made in China rather than locally produced like they are in Bressanone. Indeed, the Christmas market in Bressanone definitely emphasized artisan crafts that the Bolzano market has been lacking the past couple of years.

Of course, for me, the focus at any of these markets is not the trinkets for sale, it's the food. We had been introduced to a typical Tyrolean Christmas market while we were in Austria. We were in Innsbruck for three days that year, and we made it our mission to sample as many types of food at their Christmas Market as possible.

Well, it was for research purposes, after all.

Although we tried all kinds of things, the best by far was *gröstl*, a hearty hash browns dish, with potatoes, meat bits (e.g., small pieces of pork or ham), onions, and herbs. Delicious! We had this dish a couple of times, and also tried a version made with macaroni instead of potatoes, which was good, but the potato version was better.

Unfortunately, the food at the Bolzano Christmas market wasn't quite up to that level. For one thing, we didn't find any *gröstl* available, and that had been our favorite food at the Innsbruck market. Hmph.

As a substitute, we did try some *wurst*, at the Wurst Boutique stand. *Wurst* are essentially hotdogs of different shapes and sizes, made of various meats; they are an extremely popular festival food here in the Tyrol, perhaps the most requested version being a "wurst with sauerkraut" sandwich. We hadn't had a chance to try that in Innsbruck. Truth be told, I'm actually not a big sauerkraut fan. However, in the interest of research, I tried one of these sandwiches.

And ... I'm still not a big sauerkraut fan.

Chris tried another local specialty at the wurst stands, "curry wurst." This turned out to be *wurst* with curry powder sprinkled on it. Chris tried this so those of you who come to visit don't have to. And you do want to thank Chris for this, as it isn't anything you'll really want to try. Believe me.

The French fries we ordered as a side dish were served in a little boat-shaped cardboard box accompanied by a teeny-tiny fork. People here tend to eat the French fries with the little fork and not with their fingers. Maybe it's easier to use the fork for dipping a fry into mayonnaise, since that seems to be the "sauce" most used with the fries here.

We had much better luck with some apricot strudel that was available at the Bolzano market. The most common type around here is apple strudel, but a stand at the market offered the apricot variety, which made a nice change of pace.

Another big item on the market menu was a "Pretzel with Speck" sandwich. The pretzels around here are the soft pretzels, which come in two sizes: "big" and "even bigger." They are thick enough to cut in half length-wise like a roll and then fill with speck, the local smoked ham specialty. We didn't try it at the market, but I have subsequently purchased a pretzel at our bread shop, bought some speck, and put them together at home. Darned if that isn't a good combination. I highly recommend it. Much better than the wurst and sauerkraut sandwich, in my humble opinion. But then, I do like pretzels, and I don't like sauerkraut.

Now to drink: when you're wandering around in the cold at one of these Christmas markets, you have a selection of items to choose from. Hot mulled red wine, called *Glühwein* in German, is the primary Christmas market beverage. The German name essentially means "wine that will make you glow after you drink it." Yes, I can believe that. It's a strong mix of wine and spices, kind of like mulled apple cider, only with a strong wine instead of apple juice as the base.

There is also hot chocolate to be had, which comes both with and without rum. We tried that in Bolzano and it was pretty good, although it didn't compare to the fancy hot chocolates we could get in Vancouver at the chocolate-drink shops there. However, you can never really go wrong with a hot chocolate on a cold day.

Another popular drink on the market menus is *Bombardino*. It's like eggnog with a lot of rum, except it comes in the bottle that way, and if it's made with any eggs, they have been cooked and preserved. The markets also have regular eggnog made with fresh eggs that's a vibrant orange color, because that's the color of the yolks in the eggs around here. It's a little unsettling the first time you see it when you're used to a pale yellow eggnog. I haven't been brave enough to try it yet – maybe this year.

However, by far our favorite Christmas Market beverage is the warm, spiced orange punch, which we first tried in Innsbruck. Our favorite version of this drink at that market included the additional flavor of elderberry flowers. The orange punch was non-alcoholic; rum was optional but we didn't ever try it that way because the flavors were so tasty without it. The punch was so good that we went back to the same stall in Innsbruck three or four times over the course of three days. I'm still hoping to find a stall that makes something as tasty at the Christmas market here in Bolzano.

————————————————————

Thinking about that delicious drink at the Innsbruck market reminds me of a phenomenon you find on beverage glasses around here. All the glasses are marked with lines to indicate serving size. Wine glasses, beer glasses, water glasses, and even the mulled-wine and orange punch mugs in the Christmas markets have lines to indicate how much of the liquid is supposed to be served. For example, the Christmas market mugs used to serve the orange punch are marked with a 0.2-liters line; wine glasses are typically marked with a 0.1-liter line to show the proper serving size, and so forth.

I guess the intent is that if you order a glass of wine, for example, the line on the wine glass indicates whether they gave you the proper serving size. Maybe this came about when it became fashionable not to fill the wine glass up to the top as a serving, and this way the restaurants can show that they are giving you the "proper" amount even though the glass looks half empty.

We hadn't seen this much before we moved here, but now we see it everywhere. And what I find really funny is that now it's on all types of beverage holders, including beer glasses and even on water glasses in restaurants. For all but the wine glass I can't figure out why it's there, as the line is pretty much at the top of the water glass or punch mug, so it would seem redundant.

Anyway, whenever I see the lines on the glasses, what runs through my head is a line from an old Columbo episode. A character in that show has a habit of scratching a line on a whisky bottle with his ring to indicate how much out of the bottle he will drink; each time he does this, he says "This far … and no farther." I see those lines, and I just hear that scene in my head. Funny the random things you remember.

Oh well, we really need to get started if we're going to have time to complete all our errands this morning. The reason we've started at Piazza Walther is to patronize the best bar in town for a morning espresso before our shopping begins in earnest.

I'd say that we first became aware that Bolzano is only sort-of-like Italy when we tried to find a decent cup of espresso here. It's harder than you would think. A major disappointment for me was discovering that the bar in the building at the entrance to our apartment complex serves pretty undrinkable espresso.

Dang. I mean, reliable access to good espresso is a reasonable expectation for life in Italy, no?

Luckily, early on we discovered that Bernardo at a bar here in Piazza Walther makes the best cup of espresso in town. I most often detour here before making the rounds on the rest of my errands. Bernardo falls into the category of what I call the "people you sort of know." These are people you interact with almost every day who seem to recognize you now, but whose name you may or may not know. Of course, they don't necessarily know your name either.

Anyway, here in Bolzano, it's an interesting type of relationship, where the people I interact with every day are both friendly as well as very patient about putting up with my rather stumbling attempts at Italian.

For example, I see Bernardo, the barista at my favorite coffee bar, for just a couple of minutes each day. There's not really time to have a lengthy chat about anything, but I do want to try to practice saying something to him in Italian if I can. The only topic that readily comes to mind in this situation is the weather. But, if the weather hasn't been changing much, there's only so far you can go with that topic. But still, it's a stab at speaking Italian, and I get to feel a little more Italian when I'm having my mid-morning cup of espresso.

Before we leave Piazza Walther, I should point out that across from Walther's statue is the Bolzano cathedral, an impressive church in the Gothic style. They scrubbed the outside of it last year, and now it's clean, and in the case of the roof, gleaming. It was partially destroyed during World War II, but has been completely restored in the past few decades.

Not surprisingly, it's a real tourist magnet, and all the tour buses unload their passengers in front of the Cathedral. Which means Piazza Walther, across the street, often has clumps of those tour groups, clustered around their tour guides, scattered like moving obstacles throughout the square, as they mill around waiting for the next stop on their tour. We'll need to navigate our way around those groups as we move out of the square and head off to our next stop: the bank.

At the Bank

Before hitting the stores, we need to swing by the bank machine to get cash. From Piazza Walther, it's an easy walk around the corner to the main branch of our bank.

Usually I just use the ATMs at the bank and don't need to go inside the building. But when I have to go into the lobby and go to a bank teller for something, I most often get "Richard Gere" to help me.

Well, OK, so it's not *really* Richard Gere, it's just a guy who looks like him. But he even has a "Free Tibet" sticker on his computer, which only serves to reinforce his resemblance to the American actor.

Anyway, "Richard" is another one of those people I "sort of know." He's very patient and waits while I muddle through my questions and requests in Italian, answering me slowly, in Italian, so that I can follow along more easily. He actually speaks English better than I speak Italian, but I do appreciate his patience with letting me practice my Italian. We never talk about the weather, but he wears interesting ties, so I have learned some vocabulary in order to compliment him on his "cravatta" (that's how to say "tie" in Italian). OK, it's not a topic that leads to a lengthy conversation, but at least it's a change from the weather.

_____

We discovered early on that the notion of the "check is in the mail" wouldn't apply here in Italy, as they don't seem to use checks here. Instead, there's the concept of the *bonifico* which is a direct payment from one bank account to another; it can be between your account, and a business account or between your account and an individual's account. It's not something I had ever seen before we came to Italy. Perhaps nowadays it's possible to do this in the U.S. and Canada, but it wasn't when we lived in those countries. Arranging for a *bonifico* to be sent to someone is the main reason I ever have to go *into* the bank.

Paying the rent, for example, with a *bonifico* is really simple: we just need our landlady's bank account information, and then, at the teller window, I can tell them to transfer the money for the rent from our account into hers. I can even set it up to have it automatically paid every month. Simple. Who would have thought it – something that involves paperwork in Italy is actually easier than the same thing was in the U.S.

Of course, that's not to say that I've never had a problem at the bank. I remember once when my little ATM adventure at the bank turned out to be an interesting test of my Italian...

It was kind of like those pop quizzes I remember from school, where you'd show up for class one day and a teacher would spring an unexpected test on you, one that you hadn't necessarily prepared for.

Of course, one could argue that I have pop quizzes every

day in Italian, since I have to use it on all my daily expeditions.

But when you're trying to get your ATM card back from the ATM machine that just ate it, somehow there's much more riding on making sure you're communicating effectively with the person you're talking to. Compared with, for example, making sure that the clerk understood you wanted whole wheat bread and not rye.

Anyway, on the day in question, I had gone up to the ATM machine at the bank, the ATM that's just there to the right, outside the doors of the bank. Usually I use the one that's over there on the left, behind that a small, semi-secret door. One day I accidentally walked too close to that door, and it opened automatically, revealing a room with an ATM machine. An odd experience, actually, the first time that happened. But it certainly has turned out to be good to know that there is an indoor ATM on those days when it's snowing and blustery outside.

But I digress.

Anyway, on that particular day I used the main ATM near the front doors. And it ate my card, something that I'd luckily never had to deal with before in any country. But something that I definitely needed to figure out how to get resolved at that moment.

So I headed into the bank and talked to the friendly receptionist who sits at the desk just inside the front doors, who is yet another one of those "people I sort of know." I'm not

sure what her real job, is, but she sits at a desk by the door
and handles certain types of questions about your account.
I usually manage to mangle my syntax in my questions to
her, but she is unfailingly pleasant and friendly, and always
manages to figure out what the heck I'm talking about and
find an answer for me.

Fortunately for me, she's also bilingual in Italian and
German, which was handy when the guy in charge of the
ATM machine turned out to speak only German, no Italian
and no English.

But once we got all the linguistic logistics sorted out, he
rescued my ATM card. It turned out the machine was just
broken, and my card worked fine in the other ATM, which I
subsequently tried at the receptionist's suggestion. Whew.

After getting my card back, though, I still had to pay our
landlady a *bonifico* for the bi-monthly electric bill, so I
actually needed to go back inside to do that. Richard Gere
was busy, so I went to another guy and proceeded to
ask him to do the *bonifico* for the bill, explaining what I
needed in Italian. After having been tongue-tied over some
vocabulary in my earlier interaction with the receptionist,
it was a surprise to discover that all the right vocabulary
popped into my head at the right time. A first for me: I got
through the entire exchange without once fumbling over
the words. And it was even all pretty darn grammatical,
too.

So, a couple of small victories at the bank that day – I
got my ATM card back along with lots of applied Italian

practice. My Italian wasn't perfect, but I think earned a solid A- that day's pop quiz.

Fortunately, my ATM transactions are normally fairly straight-forward, so we won't need to have any linguistic adventures at the bank this morning. Let's withdraw some cash and get on our way with some shopping. Our first stop is just across the street from the bank: the supermarket.

Grocery Store Shopping

We should probably go over a few of the ground rules for shopping at stores in Bolzano. Shopping here is a series of ongoing lessons for learning the local cultural norms and expectations.

Later this morning we'll be doing our fruit and vegetable shopping in Piazza Erbe, the open-air market a few blocks from Piazza Walther.

Before I came to Bolzano I had read that you don't pick out the fruit and veggies yourself at those kinds of markets. Instead, you say what you want and then they pick it for you. It's not considered polite – and, indeed, it's pretty much not allowed — to go poking and prodding among the fruit and vegetables on display at the Piazza Erbe market. The vendors can get quite upset if you try to touch anything yourself.

I have observed this to be the case on many occasions. I saw a customer — who looked like a local, actually — being chewed out in Italian or German by a market worker, all for picking up a basket of berries.

Since I'd read about this in the books, I have been careful not to do that since we got here. However, it means I've had to figure out the words for stuff in advance and then try to pronounce them properly. This can be tricky. For example, the word for "peach" in Italian sounds a lot like the word for "fish" if you're not careful, but luckily the same person doesn't usually sell both, and so far people at the markets have always figured out what I really want, no matter what I mispronounce.

I also do a lot of pointing with phrases like "I'll have two of that," all said in Italian. Pointing is a wonderfully effective way of communicating, particularly when you can't just serve yourself and have to tell someone else what you want in a language you don't necessarily speak well.

I didn't point out this out earlier, but in a coffee bar, you either go up to the bar to order (like we did today) or you can just sit down at an outside table and someone will come and take your order. Or, you can do a hybrid approach: order at the bar and then indicate you'll be sitting outside.

The one thing you don't want to do is take any food yourself without first checking with the barista. For example, the frozen treats sold in a freezer case by the door should not be seen as being like a 7-11 in the U.S. See this bar over here by the entrance to the supermarket? Soon after we arrived in town, I made the mistake of going over to the freezer case there. Suddenly, a woman — who turned out to be the barista — came zooming over, talking a mile a minute in Italian and German, clearly not happy. Although she made no move to help me or get anything for me, it was clear she didn't want me doing it myself.

She was really rather rude about the whole thing, unlike other people here who seem to be more tolerant of bizarre foreigner behavior.

But it turned out that I had actually made a local faux pas by opening the case, and she had the moral high ground. According to one of Chris's colleagues, here in Italy one would never think of touching any type of food, anywhere, including at a bar/café, even if it's sitting right out in the open and seemingly inviting you to help yourself.

But, having said all that, we're about to enter one of the few places where this "look but don't touch" prohibition does NOT apply: the supermarket.

In fact, the supermarket is one store here in Italy that works much the way it does in North America: you get a shopping cart, you browse, you touch, you select what you want from the shelves or cases without waiting for someone to serve you.

However, there are some key differences to keep in mind while we're here in Despar, one of the chain supermarkets in Bolzano. This one here in the city center is the branch location I like to go to, which is one of the bigger Despar stores in Bolzano, although I'd hardly call it big by North American standards. But it is larger than the Despar store by the hotel where we first stayed, over in the Gries area of Bolzano. That location was super tiny and had a single path through the store. You entered via one aisle, which then led around to another aisle, which led to another aisle, etc. And then you were at the checkout. Kind of like a maze, but with only one route.

It was very hard to retrace your steps if you wanted to go back for anything you had forgotten, as the aisles were barely big enough for the smallish shopping carts. Invariably, I would realize as I approached the cash register area that I had forgotten something that was in the first aisle. And then I'd have to decide: is it worth navigating back through the people to get it now, or could it wait for the next trip to the market?

The bigger one here near Piazza Walther has four small aisles with things on shelves on either side of the aisle. These all lead to an open area that has a deli, a bakery, fish and meat counters and a produce section. There's a small room off that area that has wine and alcohol. The whole thing is the size of the smaller stores in North America that I've been in. Growing up, I remember thinking that the old Acme grocery store in my hometown was small, but the "big" Despar in downtown Bolzano is a fraction of the size of that old Acme.

Another small difference in the supermarket shopping experience is buying produce. Not only do you select it yourself, as you would in North American groceries, you also have to weigh it yourself in the produce section and print out a little label with the price to stick on the bag. The cashiers aren't set up to weigh stuff at the checkout like they do in the U.S. Remembering to do that on my first few trips to Despar wasn't easy, but you don't win any friends at the checkout if you have to hold up the proceedings because you forgot to get your little label on each item.

But at least it's clear where the produce section is in the store, unlike trying to figure out how to find the foods stored on the shelves in those first four aisles. The organization of the food in the store makes little sense to me.

Now, when I studied linguistics, one of the concepts we learned was the idea of a "natural class." A natural class allows you to describe sounds in languages by figuring out what features the different sounds have in common, so that the sounds can be classified together in groups – i.e. in natural classes.

If we take this concept outside the world of linguistics, we could say that groupings of things by similar characteristics are also types of natural classes. For example, hats, gloves, scarves and boots could form a natural class of cold-weather accessories.

I bring this up because the idea of what properties are common among a group of items here is (apparently) a bit different than in North America. And it's not just in supermarkets that I've discovered this. This even came up at a flea market when we purchased a music CD published by an Italian company that contained a collection of American songs from the twentieth century. On the same CD was a song by Tina Turner and another song by Fred Astaire.

Those two people did not form a natural class in my mind.

But the main place I think about this difference in natural classes is at the grocery store. I wonder, in general, whose job it is to figure out the characteristics shared by food items in order to determine how they are shelved in a grocery store. I'd never considered the matter before, and I hadn't realized how ingrained my ideas were about where to find foods in the grocery store, until I tried finding stuff in an Italian supermarket.

I was actually quite surprised at just how many supermarket food-grouping expectations I had, given that I hadn't been the primary grocery shopper for a long, long time. Chris had had that responsibility in our family for most of the 20 years we've been together, so it's really been a while since I was the primary grocery shopper, in any country. Thus, it's a little bizarre to discover I still have specific expectations of where to find things in a grocery store — and how wrong I often am when I look for something for the first time here.

For example, in a North American grocery store, I expect that there will be 1) a baking aisle with flour, sugar, oils, etc.; 2) a paper goods aisle with toilet paper and paper towels; 3) an aisle with canned goods, including vegetables, fruits, and pasta sauces 4) an aisle where you'd find cereals, crackers... etc. But why is that? What makes cereals and crackers go together as a natural class? Is it their packaging, since they are all things in a cardboard box? Their ingredients, e.g., things made with flour? I'm not certain.

Or consider, what characteristic marks something as a "baking supply"? I don't bake, but I did need to find sugar to put in our coffee at home. In North American, sugar is a baking item, grouped in the same aisle as flour, cake mixes, spices, oils, etc. But not here, where sugar is actually shelved with coffee and tea, in the same aisle as cereal, cookies, and cake mixes. Flour, on the other hand, is not there along with the sugar – flour is in another aisle. And oil is in still another aisle. So maybe it's a "things that take sugar" grouping that puts coffee and tea with sugar in the same aisle with cereal; some people do put sugar on cereal, after all. And boxes of cookies and other desserts are also in this aisle. Yes, maybe this is definitely the "things that go with sugar" aisle.

If we use that idea as our hypothesis for this aisle, it then comes as no surprise that crackers aren't there. Where are they? Well, actually they are off in the potato chips aisle.

Go figure.

Anyway, now that we've gathered our purchases in the shopping cart, we need to make our way to the checkout.

A consequence of the store layout at this Despar location is that there isn't a lot of space to line up at the checkouts. So, you wind up lining up down one of the four food aisles. Always fun when you have a cart and someone else with a cart wants to come down the aisle to get something, and you're both negotiating around the special displays of holiday cakes and cookies stacked in the middle of the aisle.

When we get to the checkout, we'll be confronted with the question about the bags. The question is not the North American "Paper or plastic?" Rather, they will want to know whether or not we want to *buy* a bag. Uniformly, the grocery stores offer reusable plastic sacks for 5 cents a bag. Or you can bring your own to use instead, which is what I usually do.

Let's see, what else to point out about the supermarket. We won't see this today, but back when we first arrived, I'd always get a handful of green stamps back with my change from the cashier. I mean "green stamps" literally: they were green and stamp-shaped.

It turned out that these functioned just like the Green Stamps I remember from when I was a kid, where you saved them up and bought merchandise with them. The program here was only a limited-time thing, which ended a few months after we arrived. And I wound up causing quite a stir trying to redeem my collected green stamps at Despar for the "bonus items" offered at the end of the promotion.

The bonus items turned out to be mainly plates and pots in the lower-points range. I hadn't really collected very many points overall, having only had a few months to get my stamps. So we didn't have enough points for anything interesting; at most we could have gotten a plate or maybe two plates unless we supplemented the points with money to purchase a bonus pot. And we didn't need anything like that. So, rather than stuff we didn't need, I opted instead for the choice to donate our points to a charity in Cote d'Ivoire in Africa that builds schools there. We had enough points to do that several times over, which was fine: worthy cause vs. unwanted plate. It seemed like a good idea at the time.

However, it wasn't such a good idea from Despar's point of view. Apparently, when you have enough points for a plate, you are supposed to get the plate. But I didn't want a plate, right? So I handed over my paper with my points, having filled out the attached card to say what I wanted. But I had too many points for the item – the donation item – that I'd chosen. So, the checkout woman conferred with the service desk woman, which involved lots of fast-conversation in Italian, so I didn't follow what they said. Then, the checkout woman, with a heavy sigh, got up and went over to the racks of boxes of bonuses, and pulled down a big cardboard box, out of which she started pulling piggy banks.

Now the piggy banks were the symbol, in the green stamps bonus book, of the donation to the charity. I hadn't realized it represented a real ceramic one; I thought it was just a symbol of giving money.

Anyway, we are now the proud owners of three blue piggy banks.

Of course, I didn't really need the piggy banks either, which I was going to explain, but then the checkout woman started to tell me that it was odd to be choosing such a small thing with all the points I had, and that this was what went with "number 26" (the donation item ID number), and that I should have chosen something else since I had more points if I didn't want the banks.

Well, I think that's what she said. At that point, she was not thrilled, the woman behind me in line was not thrilled, and the service desk woman had abandoned the whole thing all together. None of them seemed to think that making the donation with the points was a good thing, at least from what I could tell. So I just took up all the piggy banks and went on my way.

As it turned out, I didn't ever get the little receipt officially stamped to show that I'd redeemed the points for the donation. Hopefully, getting it stamped wasn't necessary in order to make sure the donation actually happened. – I'd hate to think that after all that work, the end result was only getting those piggy banks, without the charity winding up with any money!

So in the end, perhaps I should have just gotten that plate.

Anyway, all that's neither here nor there, since they don't have the green stamps promotion anymore.

We've only stopped in at the supermarket today to pick up a few small things: a box of dried pasta and some toothpaste. When I do a bigger excursion to this kind of supermarket, I take my little wheeled shopping cart so I can lug back cartons of orange juice, boxes of cereal, and maybe a bottle or two of inexpensive local wine.

While we could buy everything at the supermarket, I find that the quality isn't as good for produce, meats, cheeses, and breads. I've only taken you on this detour today so you can get a feel for this kind of shopping, which is as close to a North American shopping experience as anything gets around here.

But my typical morning shopping always involves many more stops, and luckily it's not necessary to go to the supermarket every day. So we'd better get going up the street to the Via Portici, the central shopping street in Bolzano. On the way there, we can talk a bit more about how we'll shop in the smaller stores.

Medieval Shopping Mall

The street we've come to now is the Via Portici, the biggest and oldest shopping street in Bolzano. It has been a shopping street since the twelfth century. Look up and you'll see that this narrow street has buildings on both sides that have colorfully painted porticos that overhang the cobblestone street. Beneath the living quarters on the top floor of the buildings sit the shops at street level, with covered sidewalks that protect the shoppers from the elements. All the guidebooks suggest that this area is like a modern shopping mall. Well, maybe so, but only somewhat like one, in my opinion. It has several floors of apartments in the same buildings above the stores. And, it was designed in the twelfth century, so it looks pretty medieval, even if the stores are mostly modern. It's not the same atmosphere you find at the Moorestown Mall in New Jersey, that's for sure.

I don't actually do much shopping along this street for my daily errands, although I do patronize the Farmacia Madonna, one of the oldest shops along the Via Portici; it has been operating in this location since 1602. It has frescos on the ceiling and apothecary drawers in the walls that they still use to store the packets of drugs, herbs and other things you find in a drug store.

I use that term "drug" literally, by the way. I should really call this a pharmacy in English, because it bears little resemblance to a North American "drug store".

In North America, the term "drug store" no longer means a place just for "drugs" per se, but rather refers to a bigger store that carries a whole range of items, such as over-the-counter drugs like aspirin, Tylenol and allergy medicine, as well as miscellaneous stuff like shampoo, toilet paper, cosmetics, bandages, cleaning supplies, patio furniture, electronics, etc, etc. etc. Plus a North American drug store will also have a pharmacy where you can get drugs that require a prescription.

For the over-the-counter drugs in these North American stores, you can pluck them off the shelves, reading the packages to your heart's content in order to figure out what you want before you buy it.

Let's contrast that with the experience at a *farmacia* here in Bolzano, which is the same, I believe, as what you'll find everywhere in Italy. You can only buy drugs – both over-the-counter and prescription drugs - in an Italian *farmacia* store. While this kind of shop also sells cosmetics, hand creams, shampoos and deodorants displayed on shelves in the store proper, there's no touching of those items yourself. Rather, it's another one of those "look but don't touch" shopping places.

So when you want to get something, you go to the counter and ask. If it's an item out on the shelves, a pharmacist comes out from behind the counter and gets it off the shelf for you. But if it's any kind of drug, whether prescription or non-prescription, the pharmacist gets it from behind the counter out of those little drawers you see over there. I've purchased hand cream, deodorant, band-aids, and aspirin at a *farmacia*. And, as Chris put it, the over-the-counter drugs are really, literally, that. They are always behind the counter, mostly in the drawers. So, when you buy it, they hand it to you "over-the-counter". Which I don't think was necessarily what the English term was intended to mean, but there you have it.

The system here has its benefits: you get personal service for everything, and the pharmacists are well educated in all the products, both the drugs and everything else. So, for example, when I was looking for some hand cream for very dry skin, they were able to offer advice on what to buy. Very nice.

The downside, though, at least for me, is that this is definitely not a "spur of the moment" type of shopping, since it requires extensive vocabulary research ahead of time for each new thing I need. PlusI need to be able to follow the answers in Italian, which requires even more vocabulary that I can't always prepare for in advance. These little linguistic challenges add spice to my shopping expeditions.

By the way, that prohibition against touching really extends to a wide variety of situations, including buying clothes at these small shops along the Via Portici. Most of the time I'm OK with this, but I did get a mild talking-to at one clothing shop down the way from the Farmacia Madonna, just for looking into a closet of shirts by myself. That's how the clothes were displayed in that shop, in the closets, not hanging out on racks. The idea in these shops is you wait for help and/or call over to ask them to help. You do not take anything yourself. I find this a much harder way to shop for clothes, since there's little casual browsing to be done.

In most non-clothing smaller stores, like a housewares store, I've also never had a chance to touch anything myself. The housewares stores are so crammed full of stuff that it would be almost impossible to find anything on your own, anyway. So, for any houseware buying outings, I usually try to memorize vocabulary so I can ask the salesperson for the item. Or, hope I remember enough vocabulary so that I can improvise explaining what I want if I can't remember the word.

Of course, the fall-back plan always is to say (in Italian) "just looking," then wander around and hope to spot it on the shelf. Then, I can take the salesperson over to the shelf with me, and say, "I'll take one of these, please."

Or if I can't find the exact item, but I can find something similar, that works, too, since I can say in my best Italian "I would like — " ... then pause for effect while clearly searching for a forgotten word ... then continue in Italian with ... "um, ... something like this one but for X" where X is a word related to the thing I want.

For example, in one store, after using the "I would like this" phrase to point to a sponge mop, I added that I also wanted something like that but for cleaning the toilet. But of course, despite having looked up the word for toilet bowl 10 minutes before I went to the store, I couldn't remember it, so I had to talk around it — "I'd like something like X in order to clean the thing in the bathroom that isn't the shower." I know, that's rather convoluted, but one has to work with the vocabulary one can think of at the moment.

So while my request came out sounding rather odd, it worked: the proprietor flourished not one, but two models of toilet bowl brushes for me to choose from. When I asked her which one was better, she waved the one in her right hand and said "this one, it's a Euro cheaper". Ah, a woman after my own heart. Some things are universal.

But my favorite housewares shopping story was at a place just beyond the Via Portici. I like to refer to it as "the tale of the coffee scoop."

First I should explain that there are several kinds of stores that sell household goods here. One is the "crammed full of stuff'" type of store where I bought that mop and toilet brush. Those stores have lots of basic things – and lots of things made from plastic — but nothing super fancy or expensive.

Then there are the fancy housewares stores, much more like the upscale kitchenware stores in North America. No hardware, no mops, etc., no general household things, just fancy dishes, silverware, crystal stemware, pots and pans.

I went to one of those housewares stores looking for a few things when we first moved into our apartment, including fancier wine glasses by the Riedel company that we had had in Vancouver, and which in Vancouver weren't too expensive, actually, even though they are made in Austria. I had noted while walking by this store one day that it happened to carry that brand of glassware.

Just like the not-so-fancy housewares place, it's also a no-touch shopping experience, where the proprietors pounce on you when you walk in, to see how they can help you. If you say you're just looking, they follow you around while you do.

Ultimately, I had a pretty successful trip to this fancier one, where I got a cutting board, a pot to make rice in (i.e., a pot with a tight-fitting lid since our apartment didn't come with one), and a couple of other things. My limited Italian vocabulary was holding up pretty well. I'd tried to cram the necessary vocabulary before I went and, as I've mentioned before, you can do a lot with that phrase "I want one of those" and pointing to the item if you can spot it on the shelf.

So I successfully got to the end of my list. And then proceeded to push my luck and decided to look for a little coffee scoop. I hadn't looked up the word ahead of time, but I thought I could describe it, knowing the words for spoon, *moka* (the type of coffee pot they commonly use here) and coffee. And since the little hotel apartment kitchen where we'd first stayed was outfitted with one of these scoops, I thought they must be fairly common here.

Well, the very friendly, non-English speaking shop worker who was waiting on me tried *valiantly* to figure out what the heck I meant. I mimed putting the coffee in the pot to make the coffee, explaining (I thought) that I wanted a thing like a spoon for the coffee and the pot. I did not recall at that moment how to say "to put the coffee in the pot," however. In my defense, I would like to point out I had been in Italy and learning Italian only for a month or so at that point.

Anyway, my charades technique wasn't perfect, so when all I could say was "like a spoon" and "for the coffee" while trying to illustrate the action of putting coffee in a pot, the sales woman looked confused. But then she had an "ah ha!" moment, and came back with the little spoons you use to stir the sugar in an espresso cup.

OK, well, I needed a couple of those too. And it was on the right track, but not exactly what I was looking for.

So I said no, that wasn't quite it, but it wasn't important, and I thanked her, thinking we could just stop there. But she was determined to figure this out. She went and got another sales person, who also didn't speak English. So we went through the whole mimed "like a spoon" routine again. This time the other woman came back with a *moka*. Hmm, well, I could see that they were trying to guess which part of the process I needed something for. But clearly a scoop wasn't as common as I thought for the process of loading coffee into the *moka*.

I again tried to thank them and say never mind, not important, but they were now both determined to figure this out. They went and consulted yet another sales person, who spoke a little English. And after they went through the whole thing with him, the three of them triumphantly presented me with a coffee scoop. The biggest, heaviest, fanciest coffee scooping device I have ever seen, actually. It's stainless steel, with a scoop at least the size of two tablespoons on one end, and a tamper on the other, that's flat, for tamping down the coffee in the pot like they do for espresso machines, but designed for a *moka*. The sales folks actually did their own pantomime, with a *moka* as a prop, to show me how to use it. (The odd part is that the instructions for making coffee in a *moka* always say *not* to tamp down the grounds, so I'm not sure why you need this, although the coffee scoop box clearly says it is for a *moka*.)

This uber-scoop is quite the contraption, really. And of course it's in a different scoop league than what I'd originally been thinking of. But since it wasn't too expensive, I bought it. After the sales people went to all that effort, I could hardly say no — it seemed like they should get some sort of reward for figuring out that the crazy American lady wanted a coffee scoop.

Now most of my shopping experiences aren't quite so

memorable. However, while we're paused reminiscing about my shopping adventures, let me tell you one more, which I like to call "The Razor's Quest." It's the saga of what happens when one woman, alone, sets off to buy a man's electric razor in Bolzano, Italy. You might not think of this item as the potential subject of a quest. Let me explain.

Back in February we arrived home after a weekend trip to Verona, and Chris's razor picked the next morning to give up the ghost. Well, almost - it worked, but only slightly, and it was clearly time to get a new one.

OK, I figure I can do this for him. After all, in the past I have scoped out where to buy small electronics in Bolzano. I even bought a paper shredder at one of these stores, despite the fact that I neglected to look up the Italian for "paper shredder" ahead of time. Now it's true that I ultimately bought the shredder at a little store where they had it in a box in plain sight, so I was able to say "I want to buy that," while pointing to it, always my favorite shopping tactic. However, I would like to note that in another store before that, with nary a box in sight, I had described in Italian that I wanted "a machine that broke paper into small pieces." Well, that's what a shredder does, right? Anyway, it turned out that at that store the shredders were out of stock, but the woman understood what I was looking for. At least, I think she did.

But I digress.

Anyway, the task was to purchase an electric razor, and I thought it would be simple, since I even (sort of) knew the word for razor in Italian.

In North America, my strategy would have been to try a store like K-Mart or Target in the U.S., or London Drugs in Vancouver. They don't have stores like that here, so my choices were either small electronics stores, or bigger ones, more like the old Circuit City or Best Buy in North America (in terms of the types of things they sell). In the North American stores, I would have stood in front of the shelves, picked the boxes down to read the labels, and made a choice accordingly.

Here in Bolzano, I started out by going to the smaller electronic stores first, since they are usually easier to deal with, and I like giving them business. And, they were open on a Monday morning; the bigger electronic stores, harkening back to traditional shopping hours in Italy, are closed here on Monday mornings.

A morning of pounding the pavement going to several small stores yielded surprisingly few razor choices: each place only had one or two models on display, for fantastically high prices. Would you pay $200 for an electric razor? No, neither would I. And, since I couldn't pull boxes off the shelves, I couldn't read the labels to see why these razors were so darned expensive.

Lest you think that prices here in Italy are just extraordinarily high, it turns out that the same models I saw in these stores are also super expensive on Amazon.com in the U.S. I guess the little stores I went to only stocked the high-end razors. Who knew there even *were* high-end electric razors?

Anyway, on Monday afternoon I set off for one of the "big box" stores, Euronics.

Just like any other store in Bolzano, there's no real browsing done here, with most items not available to pull off the shelf and examine on your own. But while standing in front of the shelves, I could see that they at least had many more models of razors, some at decidedly more reasonable prices. So when the saleswoman zoomed over to ask me what I wanted, I told her a *rasoio*, the Italian word I had learned for razor.

However, it turned out that the key to any razor shopping discussion here revolves around a fair amount of vocabulary beyond that simple word *rasoio*. The saleswoman, trying to be helpful, asked all kinds of questions about what I needed/wanted, but the only question I followed was whether or not my husband had a beard. Ah hah! I know that word, so I can answer that question! Yes, he has a beard.

But, wait — the type of razor she then selects from the case, based on my answer, doesn't look like Chris' old razor at all. In fact, I can see on the box she's holding that it's called a beard trimmer. I try to explain this, and she tries to explain that if my husband has a beard, this is the type of device he will want. She pantomimes some shaving with it while explaining that yes, he can both shave and trim his beard with this device.

Well, to be honest, I'm really just following the pantomiming somewhat and making educated guesses as to what she's saying since none of the words are familiar. I had no idea that electronic razors came in so many styles, with so many features and so many attachments. I just try to smile and nod and not let on that mostly I have no idea what the heck she is talking about.

It's a bit of a flashback to buying that coffee scoop, actually, even though I had thought my Italian had gotten so much better since then. It just goes to show you that specialized vocabulary is NOT your friend when you're learning a language.

Anyway, long story short, I did ascertain that I could return the one she'd recommended if my husband didn't like it. OK, yes, my Italian *had* gotten better, since I was confident I had followed at least that part of the conversation.

When later Chris says that indeed it isn't the right type of razor, I prepare for my third trip to the stores. But this time, before I head back to Euronics to exchange it, I arm myself with a list of model numbers for possible razors that would be the right model, and that also would not cost more than a small computer. I figure having the list would avoid having to answer any of the sales woman's many questions the second time around.

Except.... in Europe, it turns out that the model numbers are all different from what they are in North America. The same manufacturers are carried here, but their model numbers are all off by a number or two from my list. Since I constructed my list based on the model numbers on Amazon.com, I only had the North American models written down. So, the saleswoman, again trying to be helpful, tries to offer alternates that might match the ones on my list, and so she starts to ask those questions again, with all the words I still can't follow, about the different types of models, styles, shaving preferences, etc.

Aack. What to do.

Well, I needed to buy myself more time to look up the European models, since that would avoid the need to answer any of the saleswoman's questions. I can't even begin to guess the types of things she wants to know, so I can't possibly look up the vocabulary in advance.

So, making a mental apology to Chris, who isn't really difficult to please, I proceed to say that my husband gave me the list I have, and that I have to check with him before I buy anything not on the list. I accompany this with a shrug of the shoulders and a wave of the hands, as if to say, "What can you do, eh?"

Finally, the saleswoman and I have had a successful inter-action. I shrug, she shrugs and nods knowingly, and then she writes down the model numbers they carry so I can show it to my husband. Whew.

Heading home, a little more Internet research yields me the correspondence between Panasonic model numbers in North America and Europe. I have cracked the code and am ready to go back to the store.

But by this time it is Tuesday afternoon.

Now, that weekend trip I said we'd just returned from?

It was for the Carnevale celebration that takes place the weekend before Fat Tuesday. And so, it was now Fat Tuesday. This being Italy, all shops — including Euronics — were closed that afternoon.

So the following day, on my fourth attempt to buy the razor, I go back to Euronics, show my selected model number to the sales woman and finally buy ... drum roll, please ... a razor.

See, all that work to buy something that seemed so simple. I really think this qualifies as a quest.

———————————————————————————

Back here on the Via Portici, let's walk down a little ways until we come to what looks like a hallway into one of the buildings. As I mentioned, the buildings date from the middle ages, when shopkeepers lived in the apartments above their shops. As you can see, the buildings are built quite close together, and are also quite deep, stretching back to cover the whole distance between the streets on either side. They built a series of clever internal passageways — the hallway-like passage we've come to — that run between the buildings. If you look up, you'll note that these are uncovered at the top in order to allow more light and air into the apartments that are at the top of the winding stair-cases we find in the middle of the passageway. There are also overhead, enclosed passageways that provide covered walkways to get from building to building as well, so you don't have to go down to the street level if you want to go visit your neighbor in the next building over. Quite a clever system, eh?

Some of the passageways today also contain gardens and cafes, including one of my back-up places to get a morning coffee when my favorite bar in Piazza Walther is closed. We'll stroll past it as we take the rest of this passageway over to our next stop, a wine shop on Via Streiter.

Eating and Drinking all'italiana

Here we are on Via Streiter, which runs parallel to Via Portici. This is another one of the older streets in Bolzano, retaining its medieval character with a cobblestone pavement and several sixteenth century arched "bridges" that loom overhead, spanning the width of the street. The bridges are more of those enclosed overhead passageways; these particular ones connect the Via Portici buildings to the houses on the other side of the Via Streiter. Turning left onto Via Streiter from the passageway we just came from, we'll pass by the old town hall building – there's a plaque to mark it, although only the façade is original, the rest of the building is a newer variation on the original design.

We've headed up the street to go to an *enoteca*, which is what you call a wine shop in Italy. Unlike liquor stores in the U.S., it's more than just a place where you buy alcohol – well, for one thing, it really only sells wine and maybe a few spirits, but no beer, nor anything else, as far as I know. Plus, there's a little bar area where you can get a glass of wine and maybe a tiny sandwich to munch on while you have a quick chat with your friends. People stop and do this at all hours of the day, morning, noon and night; they pop in for a small drink and visit and then go on their way.

We've just come here today to buy a bottle of wine to take home. The South Tyrol has its share of good wines, and I think we'll pick up a nice bottle of Lagrein, a local, full-bodied red wine that Chris and I like a lot. There are several vineyards dotting the hillsides around town, and there's even one down the street from this wine shop; yes, it's a vineyard located right in the center of the city.

The grapes used in each region in Italy may produce different types of wines, but every region has a fine tradition of producing good wine. This particular *enoteca* has a good selection of nice wines from all over Italy, which is fun when we want to branch out from the local varieties. Many little shops around here only sell the wines produced in our Aldo Adige province, but if you're looking for a good Chianti from Tuscany, for example, this is the shop to come to.

Actually, one thing we find striking in Italy is that you don't typically find a range of non-regional foods in shops or even in restaurants; it's usually the case that restaurants only have food from their own particular area. So, for example, in the city of Verona, the restaurants serve foods typical of the region around Verona, not foods from anywhere else.

Here in Bolzano, given its history, it's not surprising that most of the food at the restaurants is actually South Tyrolean and not Italian. Well, you know what I mean; strictly speaking, of course, South Tyrol has technically been also "Italian" for over 90 years.

But strikingly, it was here on this historically very Tyrolean Via Streiter that one day we happened upon on a really good Sardinian restaurant. That's the restaurant where we got a lesson about something I had always thought of as a cheese. Let me explain.

The Sardinian restaurant is a small place that's a bit cavern-like: you walk down a long flight of stone steps to get to its basement location. There are only seven tables, but we timed it right that first time to get one of them even though we didn't have a reservation. The menu looked interesting, and following our strategy for small restaurants, we asked the waiter/owner if he could recommend some things for us to try that were typical of Sardinian food. He was a friendly character, joking around with Chris in Italian right from the beginning.

It was a very enjoyable meal that at times felt more like we were visiting someone's house. When we were offered the standard after-dinner espresso, what we got was made and brought to the table in a little moka pot, just like we use at home, rather than being made in a fancy espresso machine like most other restaurants here use.

After we had our coffee, the owner offered to get us a typical Sardinian liquor to top off the meal, just like friends offer us liquors after dinner in their houses.

The Sardinian food we ate was simple, but very good. We had some interesting dumplings made out of potatoes, with cheese and mint mixed in that gave them a really nice, delicate flavor. We also had an interesting salad, with arugula (a popular dark-green lettuce), cherry tomatoes, and a "salted ricotta." What was interesting was that the ricotta was in slices, like a hard cheese, and not the soft ricotta that I would use to make lasagna in North America.

When the owner came to clear the plates from that course, Chris commented, in Italian, that we had really enjoyed the cheese. And the owner said, "It wasn't cheese, it was ricotta."

Wait a minute. It's "ricotta," but it's not "cheese"? What's up with that?

After further research at home on the Internet, we learned that the distinction is caused by both how it is made and what it is made from. Ricotta, despite what we've always called it in the U.S., is not considered a cheese here in Italy, since technically ricotta is made from whey, a by-product of making cheese. Therefore, ricotta is not cheese.

Now you know.

That Sardinian restaurant has become one of our favorite spots in town when we want some Italian food. It is funny, here we are technically living in Italy, but we often — only half-jokingly— find ourselves bemoaning the fact that's it's hard to find good Italian food in Bolzano.

When we need a good pasta fix, we do have a spot we go to, over near the hotel where we first stayed. It's not here in the city center, but just a short walk over to the Gries area on the edge of town.

The first time we went to this particular restaurant we actually had both a Tyrolean meat plate, and a hot (temperature-wise) pasta dish served with a cold tomato sauce on the side. Both the food and the fact that the restaurant served both Tyrolean and Italian food were good and interesting.

The owner was quite a likeable character, another one who enjoyed bantering back and forth with Chris in Italian. We enjoyed it and have continued to go back, even now that we don't live next door.

After that first time, we started asking the owner to suggest something for us to eat, rather than our picking from the menu. This really seems to be a good strategy for getting whatever is freshest that day at all the little restaurants in Italy. One of our favorite dishes there is something that the chef came up with - a seemingly simple pasta dish with tomatoes, spicy little red peppers, black olives, olive oil, and garlic. He also makes a great spaghetti dish with various green vegetables, some *borlotti* beans (kind of like a kidney bean only light brown), and a little bit of spicy pepper. Yum.

We try to go back there at least once a month. The food is basically Italian home cooking: simple, tasty and satisfying.

And we also enjoy interacting with the owner – he's a friendly character, another one of those people you "sort of know", although we do know his name now. And we know his twin brother, since he's the chef for all the delicious meals that we eat there. Definitely one of our favorite spots for an Italian meal in Bolzano.

When we want a simple bite to eat that's Italian and closer to where we live now, we head to another spot in the center of town that has wonderful Italian food. It's run by two brothers from Puglia, in southern Italy, and they serve up specialties from that region. The brothers' restaurant isn't really a restaurant; it's a combination wine bar/pizza place/photography gallery. An unusual combination, to be sure, but a really fun place to go. Of course, in the interest of full disclosure, I should mention that yes, this is the place that has asked Chris and me to do several photo exhibitions since we've lived here. So we may now have a slight bias in favor of its odd mix of food, wine, and photos.

Anyway, one of my favorite things on the menu is a potato pizza; that is, it's a pizza with potatoes as a pizza topping, not a pizza where potatoes form the pizza crust. When we saw a potato pizza on the menu, we didn't think those two items would go together well, but they do. The potatoes are thinly sliced, mixed with sausage, rosemary, salt, olive oil, and then spread out on top of the pizza dough. It's a "white" pizza: i.e., no tomatoes or tomato sauce, just a little mozzarella under the potatoes. There's also a version without the mozzarella, where the flavor of the rosemary really shines through. Very tasty.

With all the fancy pizzas we used to get at our favorite pizza place in California years ago, we'd never run across one with potatoes before. Sometimes, it's the simple things that are the best, eh?

They have many wonderful dishes at this place, and you can even make reservations for special fish and other typical Pugliese-style Italian dishes. All of which we have tried more than once. In the name of research, of course. We're dedicated to our food research, as you know.

It has also become the place where we now go for our "anniversary" pizza topped with speck, the Tyrolean smoked ham that's ubiquitous in these parts. I think I mentioned it back when we were talking about those pretzel sandwiches at the festivals.

Because we had arrived in Bolzano on a Sunday, most restaurants — and all stores — were closed. For dinner that first night, we happened upon a pizza place that was open and offered a pizza with speck. And thus a tradition was born: a pizza with speck to mark the anniversary of our arrival in Bolzano. It seems a fitting food to celebrate living in this area: it's Italian but with a Tyrolean twist.

Of course, now we know that our favorite pizzeria/wine bar is really the best place to get it. For this year's speck pizza, the Pugliese chef's suggestion was a "pizza bianca" - a white pizza without tomato sauce, topped with speck (of course), plus a firm white cheese from Puglia called *cacciacavallo* and ... apples. Chris and I both thought the apples sounded odd for a pizza, but the chef is quite talented, so we gamely tried it. And boy, was it tasty!

So first we discovered the delicious combination of potatoes on pizza at this place, and then we found out there is a wonderful pizza to be had there with speck and apples as well – who knew these unusual combinations would work so well together? Definitely, we have found the right place to go for our pizza here in Bolzano.

While we're on the subject of pizza, let me add one final note. Here in Italy, when you order pizza, everyone gets their own pizza, and eats it with a knife and fork. The typical size of the pizza pie is anywhere from 10-12 inches, which is bigger than a typical North American "personal pan" pizza, I think. The pizza crust they make here is super thin. And, obviously, the toppings are not just your standard toppings. It's definitely a world away from a greasy North American fast-food pizza with its typically doughy, undercooked crust.

Thank goodness.

Ah, I believe I've digressed quite a bit again, haven't I. Here I am *talking* about food, and we should really be getting back to our errands to *buy* some food this morning. Actually, all that talk about speck puts me in a mind to buy some. So, now that we've got our wine, let's turn right out of this *enoteca* and take the first left, which will take us into the Piazza Erbe, the fruit and vegetable market here in Bolzano.

What, you don't think that's an obvious place to go to buy some speck? Well, come right this way and let me show you.

More than just Speck

OK, so here we are at the top of Piazza Erbe, just around the corner from the enoteca where we bought the wine. Although called a *piazza*, it's really more of a long street that's slightly wider than the normal streets in the center of town. It's been a thriving marketplace since Roman times (supposedly); the current fruit and vegetable market design dates back to the Middle Ages. Today the street is lined on both sides by 20 or so vendors selling their wares from green metal stalls topped by retractable white awnings

There are also stores in the buildings behind the stalls, and as we walk along the street we'll come to two different meat delis located on our left. The first one I always refer to as the "old lady deli" as I always see lots of little old ladies heading down the steps into that store to buy their meats in the morning. Inside, it's more than a little intimidating for me. The clientele is clearly only locals, and the staff expects you already to know what every piece of meat on display is – there are no labels on anything in the long, glass cases that make up the two counter areas. I will go there only if I'm feeling particularly brave, since it's a challenge for me to tackle ordering.

Instead, I usually go to the shop next door, which is where we'll head right now. It's a tiny *salumeria*, a word I think must just mean "place that sells pork products," since that's pretty much all it sells. There's salami, already-cooked roast pork, and of course, that locally famous smoked pork called speck.

I really like this shop – it's run by a young married couple who are another two of those people I "sort of know." Like the other people in this category, this couple is super-friendly and adept at figuring out my (mis)pronunciations of the names of the meats and cheeses they sell. If they aren't busy waiting on anyone else, they will also usually anticipate my basic order and have two packets of sliced speck ready as I walk in the door.

―――――――――――――――――――――――――

Now this shop is exactly the place you'd want to go to in order to buy all the styles of meat you'd need for a *Törggellen*, the big harvest feast that's a tradition here in the South Tyrol. Unlike Thanksgiving in North America, where everyone celebrates on the same day, there is no one day for the Törggellen; restaurants offer these meals throughout the autumn.

I think of it has a harvest celebration, but I don't know whether that's really an accurate description, because the focal point of the meal is on the meat platter, which has many types of pork —and only pork— as the meat of choice.

But before you get to the meat, the Törggellen meal begins with a first course, with your choice of several items. For example, you might start with *schlutzkrapfen*, little squares of pasta that look like thin ravioli, typically filled with "something green" as Chris puts it.

I love these things; Chris not so much. This dish is always topped with melted butter and Parmesan cheese; really, what's not to love.

Or you might start with *canederli*, big bread-based dumplings. These are made with bread-for-stuffing like you'd put in a turkey, only it's shaped into balls or ovals and then mixed with cheese, and/or speck, and/or spinach. Like the previous dish, *canederli* are often served in a melted butter sauce and topped with Parmesan cheese.

After the first course, the Törggellen feast is all about the meat. They bring out a huge platter filled with many types of pork-based products. There were at least four kinds of pork products piled on the platter at the *Törggellen* we went to; I couldn't even begin to identify all the types we had.

Here at the *salumeria* it's possible to buy smoked pork sausage, white pork sausage, fresh pork sausage, pork sausage with herbs, etc. etc.. all "house-made" by the folks at this shop. They also have a range of sausages made from other animals, too; my favorite is the wild boar sausage, but the one made from donkey meat isn't bad either.

The most different of all the foods we ate at the *Törggellen* was the dark red *blutwurst* sausage.

In English, the literal translation of that is "blood sausage," but I read on the Internet that in England this is also called "black pudding." I'd never tried anything quite like it before.

The tradition here in the South Tyrol is to serve it whole and hot; you slice off a bit of it when you serve yourself from the platter at the Törggellen. The one we had wasn't very solid and sort of fell apart and spilled out of the casing when you cut into it. It was really flavorful. They used a lot of spices, including cloves, which gave it a really distinctive taste. Very different and very good.

A traditional dessert at a *Törggellen* meal is another kind of ravioli-type *krapfen*, except it's deep-fried and filled with something sweet, and then topped with powdered sugar.

Roasted chestnuts are also traditional at this time of year, and are served as a final dessert at the end of a proper Törggellen. Actually, you can probably smell them right now, can't you? It's the scent of the chestnut wars here in Piazza Erbe. OK, maybe I exaggerate just a little, but seriously, things are heating up – literally - in Piazza Erbe this year with the arrival of multiple roasted chestnut vendors.

First, there was the original one, which is associated with one of the normal fruit and vegetable stalls in Piazza Erbe. He's been doing this for years.

Then, there came a rogue vendor — not someone associated with the regular stalls in the market. He set up a stall across the way from the original one last year, next to a dried-fruit vendor. He very loudly hawks his wares and jiggles the chestnuts in the pan a lot, to the annoyance of many of the other vendors in Piazza Erbe who have to listen to that all day.

Last year, the dried fruit vendor was pretty annoyed with the rogue chestnut guy for setting up his stand so close by. So, this year, the dried fruit guy had *his* relatives set up a new rival stand across the way.

So now, all the chestnut vendors are jockeying for tourist euros in pretty much the same place, clustered at or near the main intersection that runs through Piazza Erbe. They all seem to be doing brisk business, though – the cool temperatures we have here must help sell the merits of buying a hot bag of those temptingly fragrant roasted chestnuts.

Were we to stop back here in the afternoon, we'd see that there's a large cloud of smoke that settles over Piazza Erbe by the end of the day, now that there are three vendors with roasters to generate it. It covers the rest of the Piazza Erbe vendors in a gentle haze; think of it as one of the picturesque signs of autumn in Bolzano.

But fortunately, since it's still relatively early, we won't have to make our way through the smoke as we go over to get some fruit at the stall of my favorite Piazza Erbe vendor.

Fruit and Veggies

When we moved to Europe, I wondered if I'd be shopping every day at the open-air markets, just like you see in the movies. That's a stereotype I had as a North American about life in Europe.

Two years later, and what do you know – I do shop (almost) every day at the outdoor market in Piazza Erbe here in Bolzano. I don't shop there on Sundays because it's closed, along with all the shops here in town. That's probably been the hardest thing to get used to, actually: shops are closed Saturday afternoons and all day Sunday, and many also still close down in the middle of the day during the week.

The near-daily shopping has been a fun thing to do, but probably only because I'm not working and have the time to do it. It's less fun to do in the pouring rain ... or in the snow. Odd, they never show *that* in those movies.

But it is certainly true that a stop at my favorite fruit stand in Piazza Erbe is by far the highlight of my morning errands, no matter what the weather.

———————————————

The first time I bought produce at the Piazza Erbe market, I got fruit at a stand where the vendor was so friendly and pleasant, and the fruit so fresh and flavorful, that I just continued to go back to her for my fruit. Even when I didn't really know the names of the fruits early on, Hanna, my friendly fruit-stand lady, was always very patient, allowing me to stumble through my questions in Italian before she made her suggestion for what fruit was freshest to buy that day. At one point in those first few months, when I started asking her more questions about the local fruit, she commented that my Italian seemed to be improving. I think that just meant I wasn't mispronouncing the fruit names as much anymore, and I was also able (mostly) to remember the correct grammatical gender for lemon. But it was still nice of her to say.

Hanna has been selling fruit here at the market for 20-30 years now; she and her husband originally ran the stall together, but he died about 10 years ago. So now she runs it by herself. She mostly sells seasonally fresh fruits, but she always keeps some apples on hand for the tourists, even out of season. Bolzano and the surrounding valley are known for the apples grown here: this area is reportedly the largest apple producing place in all of Europe, although the types they grow here do not seem very exotic, such as Fuji and Red Delicious. But still, tourists expect apples to be available when they come here.

Hanna also carries all kinds of fruit from all over the world. By law she has to have signs with the fruit saying both what it is, in German and/or Italian, and also where it is from. Many times on the signs she'll add other comments about the fruit; for example, this summer the signs next to the strawberries promised that they were "flavorful" and "sweet," in both German and Italian.

Actually, in German one of the things it promised was that they were *aromatisch*. I'm not sure if that word conveys exactly the same idea of "scent" that its English cognate, "aromatic," does. But if it does, that may help explain why Hanna is constantly having to remind people what her other signs say: these signs prohibit touching and smelling the fruit, in three languages, German, Italian, and English.

When I first started going to the market, I thought Hanna had put "don't smell" on the sign as a kind of joke. But no, I have now witnessed people attempting to stick their noses right in the baskets to take a whiff of the merchandise on display. It drives Hanna crazy; apparently there are a fair number of people each day who do that — or try to — despite the sign. This, in addition to the people who want to poke and prod everything, and/or disturb the carefully piled pyramids of peaches, etc. by selecting from the bottom of the pile. Being an outdoor fruit vendor here has its challenges.

Since we have Hanna to recommend the best fruits on offer each day, Chris and I are completely spoiled and have a delicious fresh fruit course with both lunch and dinner. So good! I never could pick out consistently good fruit on my own, and for those two months when Hanna is closed during the winter, our fruit intake definitely suffers, since I have to get it at another stand where they don't pick the good stuff out as well as Hanna does.

By the way, I always stop and chat with Hanna quite a bit each day, so be prepared to stop here for longer than we do at any other place today. She's quite friendly and personable, and extremely patient with my Italian. This is both great fun for me to have a chance to chat with her, as well as being a great opportunity to explore different conversational topics for which I may or may not have looked up the Italian words in advance. She's very willing to let me attempt to explain things in Italian, even if I often fumble to think of words that I'm not quite sure of.

Hanna has also introduced me to all the types of fresh fruits that are available here in Bolzano.

For example, although it's a little late in the year for us to see them in the market today, in late summer and early autumn, a vast assortment of grapes turn up in the market. The vineyards are full of them at that time of year, of course, and the ones that aren't used for wine are sold to be eaten at the table. Each week seems to bring another new variety to the market stalls.

Hanna, of course, carries all the best types. One day she pointed out some small, purple grapes to me and said they were called *uva fragola* in Italian; the literal translation of that would be "strawberry grapes."

No, I don't know why the name in Italian has anything to do with strawberries. In the U.S., this type of grapes is called Concord. When I looked it up in both the English Wikipedia and the Italian Wikipedia, I learned that Concord grapes are native to the Americas and were brought over to Italy in the early 1800s. However, the American name Concord comes from a particular type in Concord, Massachusetts, which was cultivated by Ephraim Wales Bull in the mid-1800s.

Anyway, the first time these appeared at Hanna's stall, she handed me a couple to taste. The expression "bursting with flavor" came to mind — these grapes are super sweet with an intense blast of grape flavor. Irma then asked me if I was familiar with them as a grape. So I nodded, and said yes, and that I even remembered that once, when I was a kid, I helped my grandmother pick some from a wild vine in their yard, and together we made jelly from them.

I was saying all that in Italian, and since they don't actually have a "jelly/jam" word distinction like we do in the U.S., I used the word for jam, *marmellata*, which would also be used in Italian for the food product that we call "jelly" in the U.S.

And Hanna gave me a look and said, no, you don't make *marmellata* from these grapes. As in, one does not ever make *marmellata* from these grapes.

Well, if you take *marmellata* to mean only jam, i.e. a thick juice and sugar mixture with suspended pieces of fruit in it, then it's true, I've never seen grape jam like that. So I tried to explain in Italian what the difference was between "jam" and "jelly" in the U.S., thinking this would clear things up.

And Hanna still shook her head and said, no, you don't make anything like that with these grapes. She explained you can eat them raw, you can press them for fresh juice, and you can make a sweet wine out of it. But never, ever would you make anything like *marmellata* from them. They just aren't good for making that kind of thing, she said. She clearly thought I was totally confused about making *marmellata*.

And it's true, I'm no expert. The one and only time I ever made jelly was that single incident on one hot and humid summer's day with my grandmother, when we got ourselves and the kitchen covered in sticky grape remains while trying to squeeze the juice from the grapes.

But I was certain we really did we used Concord grapes. Honest.

And besides, even if I don't know how to make jelly, I do know that in the U.S. you *do* make grape jelly from Concord grapes. But it suddenly struck me that here in Italy, where they seem to make jams out of almost every fruit and vegetable (pumpkin jam, anyone?), they don't make jam out of the *uva fragola* version of Concord grapes, which in the U.S. is one of the most popular fruits from which to make jam. Er, jelly.

As it turns out, they don't make jam out of *any* type of grapes here, for that matter.

Now I haven't read up on the details of the process developed by Mr. Bull and Mr. Welch (and Mr. Smucker, later) in the 1800s, but clearly it wasn't as easy as you'd think it might be to make grape jelly. Maybe it's a property of the grape variety invented by Mr. Bull that allows the jelly to be produced? Interesting to discover that this process is actually fairly complex. I had never thought of anything to do with grape jelly as complicated, but it took a couple of clever inventors to come up with how to make it.

Well, they had the right inspiration, I guess. After all, what could be more essential to a peanut butter sandwich than grape jelly? What food would millions of school children in the U.S. have to take to lunch, if they didn't have their PBJ sandwiches, after all.

However, I think I'll hold off trying to explain that part to Hanna. They don't have peanut butter here in Italy either.

Anyway, when you meet Hanna, it's not a problem that you don't speak Italian if we decide to stay and chat. When my in-laws came to visit, about nine months after we arrived in Bolzano, I took them with me on my daily errands, just as I'm taking you today. I introduced them to Hanna in Italian, and said, in Italian, that my in-laws spoke English but no Italian. Imagine my surprise when she not only greeted them in English, but also carried on a lengthy conversation with them in perfect English. I had had no idea she could speak English like that. It turns out she's studied English at night for years and years. Amazingly, she never once got so frustrated with my Italian that she switched to English, even back when I could barely put a sentence together in Italian. I asked her later about that — in Italian — and she said she just figured that I should get as much practice speaking Italian as I could, so that I could get better more quickly.

She's such a very nice lady to allow me to do that.

Of course, Hanna's interest in learning English, and her knowledge of some English terms, has occasionally led me into having friendly discussions on topics that prove a little impossible to resolve in any language.

It all started innocuously enough. Chris and I had decided to make pancakes for a few of Chris' colleagues one Saturday. So when, on the Friday before, Hanna asked me what I was doing on Saturday, I said I was going to try making American-style pancakes.

And then she asked what pancakes were.

Now, as I said, Hanna actually speaks English fairly well, although she and I always speak in Italian. She wasn't familiar with the word "pancake", though, and there wasn't a good corresponding term in Italian that I could think of - an Italian frittata is a little bit different.

So I decided to describe how you make pancakes, thinking that might help explain what they were. To start, I said, you cook them in a skillet, a word I happened to know in Italian; I wasn't about to try to explain what a "griddle" is. I said pancakes were round (more or less) and flat like a — well, hmm, that's a good question, like a what? I still need to look up the equivalent expression in Italian for describing something as flat since the English "flat as a pancake" didn't really suggest a way to explain this in Italian.

Anyway, pancakes are flat. And made with flour, milk, baking powder, an egg .... — I got to that point, and Hanna had an epiphany; she interrupted and said, oh, I see, you're making an omelette.

Uh, no, actually. An omelette is something different, I confidently explained, made with eggs. But a pancake is made primarily with flour; it has an egg in it, but it's nothing like an omelette.

But then Hanna appropriated my own line of reasoning, saying triumphantly, but an omelette is made with both eggs and flour.

Hmm. Suddenly, I'm flashing back to the whole grape jelly debacle — er, discussion — when I'd been trying to persuade her that in the U.S. one really did make jelly from Concord grapes. So, I should have realized in that moment that I was not going to convince her that what we call an omelette in

English does not have any flour in it, and that a pancake is really not the same as an omelette in North America.

Of course, I should have realized this, but did I stop there? Oh no, because I figured I had another obvious difference to point out which would solve this for once and for all: an omelette would not be topped with a sweet syrup, whereas a pancake is (almost) always served that way in the U.S. So, clearly, omelettes and pancakes must two different things, right?

However, at this point I crucially needed to remember the word for "maple" in Italian, or even in German, since the fancy, imported-from-Canada maple syrup we were able to buy at a natural foods store here in Bolzano was labeled in German. My mind, unfortunately, drew a complete blank at that moment, however, and I couldn't figure out how to tell her what maple syrup was. After first trying, unsuccessfully, to describe the shape of a maple leaf in Italian, in order to tell her the kind of tree the syrup comes from, I realized the maple leaf is the symbol on the Canadian flag. Hanna's business associate, who is Pakistani, recognized what I was talking about when I mentioned the Canadian flag, and then he told her the word for "maple" in Italian.

Then I tried to explain that the sweet syrup comes from the tree. Not from the leaves, mind you, which is what she initially thought, given that I spent so much time trying to describe the blasted shape of the leaves in order to try to get her to figure out the name of the tree.

How *do* I get myself into these situations?

But in the end, her business partner and I convinced her that this kind of tree has a sweet syrup inside the tree that is used on top of the pancakes.

Unfortunately, I also said that the syrup is really sweet, like a really sweet sugar, and after all, you'd never put *that* on an omelette, right?

And then Hanna replied that her favorite kind of omelettes are in fact topped with butter and sugar.

I was temporarily struck dumb by a vision of maple syrup being poured over a cheese omelette. Blech. Years ago, as an exchange student in England, I completely nauseated my host sister by talking about peanut butter and jelly sandwiches, not realizing that in England, jelly refers to what we call "Jello" in North America. My imagining what a maple syrup-topped cheese omelette would be like must be my host sister's cosmic revenge for that horrific PBJ moment I had inadvertently caused her 30 years ago...

In any case, to say I wasn't going to win this debate with Hanna was an understatement, so I finally just let it go.

Later that night, Chris and I looked up terms for pancake and omelette in various languages. In Italian, a *frittata* is sort of like an omelette, but, unlike a pancake, a *frittata* is not always made with flour, and even when made with flour, a _frittata _only has a little, not a lot of flour. Further, an omelette, according to Wikipedia, is made with eggs, but does not contain any flour, ever.

So that Friday night, I decided that I just wasn't explaining something correctly in Italian when talking to Hanna about the pancakes, since pancakes weren't omelettes, but I hadn't been getting that point across to her.

Saturday dawned, and Chris and I had our pancake brunch, to which we had invited five guests, among them two Germans and two Italian-speakers (one from Tuscany, one from Bolzano), plus one local person from a town near Bolzano. The two Germans were familiar with something similar to North American pancakes in the style of what, in U.S. restaurants, is always called a German pancake: thin, small, and served with applesauce. Similar to, but not the same as American pancakes. The two Italian speakers couldn't think of any Italian food that was like the American pancakes, although they did think that sometimes a frittata will be made with a little bit of flour, but it's not really similar to a pancake.

All four of those guests also agreed that for them, an omelette is made with eggs, never with flour.

But the other guest for brunch was, as I said, from this region, and like Hanna, a German-speaker from the South Tyrol. And this last guest said that if she had to give a name to the pancakes that she'd just eaten, she'd call them … omelettes.

In my own defense, everyone else at the table, including the Italian-speaker from Bolzano/Bozen, was surprised, too.

But clearly, I owe Hanna an apology, and maybe even a batch of pancakes — er, omelettes — one of these days.

In any case, it's the highlight of my morning to stop by, talk with her, and watch her interact with the other regular customers as well as visitors to her stall. Through her I get a glimpse into the busy world of life at the Piazza Erbe market.

Now that we've left Hanna's stall, we will head down past the chestnut vendors to stop at my usual vegetable stand. I have to go there for veggies, since Hanna sells only fruit. There are six-eight vegetable stalls, but I usually go to the same one, second on the left after the intersection in the middle of Piazza Erbe when coming from Hanna's. Like many of the stalls in this market, it's staffed mostly by family members.

This is where I come for my vegetable needs: in season I'll buy asparagus, tomatoes, green peppers, red peppers, maybe some lettuce, broccoli, onions, ginger, plus fresh herbs such as basil and parsley. A quick side note: parsley is called *prezzemolo* in Italian, and I buy it often enough, but I can never get the pronunciation quite right with the stress in the right place. But the guys at this stand are patient, and they always figure out what I mean. Someday I'll master this; it's [pre-ZEM-ah-lo], not [pre-zem-AH-lo]. Sigh – you'd think I could remember that when I'm in the market.

I also buy fresh mushrooms of all types here, depending on
the season. The most popular types grown here are called
finferli in Italian – in English we call then chanterelles.
Long, thin and yellowish-brown with a small cap on top,
they are really popular in these parts. We've tried them at
restaurants in a pasta dish made with *finferli*, olive oil and
garlic. By far the best example of this dish was at a little
bar/cafe across the street from Chris' office. Sadly, it's now
out of business, but we still haven't had a better version
of the *finferli* mushrooms over pasta. At the time, we told
the chef/owner how her dish had been so far superior to
the other versions of it that we'd had before. And she
said something about the difference being in getting male
or female mushrooms. Unfortunately, I didn't quite catch
what the exact tip was regarding that — which ones to use,
and/or if it's better to use a mix. So, I've been unsuccessful
at buying the right kind to replicate this meal to date. Ah
well.

This talk about mushrooms reminds me that we saw a
bizarre story in the La Republica newspaper about the
sudden dangers of looking for wild mushrooms. The head-
line was "Mushroom Hunter Massacre!" Over a 10-day
period this past August, 19 (!) people died while gathering
mushrooms on the slopes of the mountains around here.

It seemed that this year's weather had been producing a
bumper crop of wild mushrooms on the slopes of the Alps,

which was attracting more people than usual to go and search for the perfect mushrooms. Unfortunately, some-how this led to more people than usual failing to notice that there was often a rather steep drop – nay, precipice – between them and the mushroom they were trying to pluck. So an extraordinary number of these mushroom hunters had accidentally stumbled or slid off the cliffs to their deaths.

Well, at least that's what the authorities think is happening to explain the deaths. But actually, except in one case, no one has actually seen any of these folks take their tumbles.

In the La Republica story, in addition to cautioning people to wear appropriate footwear, the experts said that it was important to always go mushroom hunting with at least one other person. But in fact, almost everyone who died had done just that. Indeed, most of the people who died had originally set off with their husband or wife, with the survivor explaining later that they'd been separated from the other while on the mountain.

Hmmm.

Now, with no disrespect intended for the poor people who died, I must say that this really has all the makings of one heck of a murder mystery. Nineteen deaths within ten days, and all but one happened with no witnesses to the "accident"? And it's mostly husbands and wives involved?

OK, maybe I read too many mystery stories, but this just seems like a twist on the usual plot involving poisonous mushrooms as a murder weapon. I mean, how many times have you read *that* in a mystery story, eh?

Another theory: somebody nefarious has been trying to protect something criminal on the mountains, and the unfortunate mushroom hunters who wandered alone and too close to whatever secret is stashed there have gotten bumped off by said nefarious person.

This idea, while somewhat as farfetched as the first one, apparently also occurred to a writer at Reuters, based on the article (in English) that appeared about this. The Reuters version describes how some of the mushroom hunters wear camouflage outfits, hunting for the mushrooms under the cover of darkness in order to protect their prized mushroom patches from being discovered.

Oddly enough, the Reuters piece says its article is based on that same La Republica article we first saw, which contains none of those camouflage details. But if you want to develop a plot where people are killing mushroom hunters to protect something, those details do go along nicely with that theory.

Then again, it was probably just a tragic series of accidents happening all at once. People do tend to tumble off the mountains while hiking around here with unfortunate regularity; it seems like there's a story about someone doing that almost every weekend. It's just usually not one person every other day on average. So it does make you wonder what's going on with the mushroom hunters on the mountains.

Personally, I'm content to do my own mushroom "hunting" here in the market as part of my everyday expeditions.

OK, let's see, how are we doing on the errands. Speck — check. Fruit — check. Veggies — check. OK, looks like we're ready to pop by the *paneficio* — the bread shop — for some bread. While I don't get that stereotypical baguette that you see in those European movies I mentioned, I do buy fresh bread every day for lunch. So, let's head in the direction of my preferred *paneficio* now.

In the Neighborhood of the Most Famous Resident of Bolzano

Actually, my favorite bread shop usually has those delicious soft pretzels that make a great speck sandwich, so let's see if they have any of those today; if not, we'll just get some other sort of fresh bread. A *paneficio* sells mostly breads, in all shapes and sizes. Rye is the popular form around here, but they also sell white, wheat, stuff topped with sunflower seeds, whole grains, etc. They also sell a few pastries, but for pastries you really need to go to a *pasticceria*, which sells cakes, cookies, strudel (particularly apple strudel, which is famous in these parts). Indeed, a *pasticceria* sells everything sweet a bakery in the U.S. might sell, except it doesn't sell any bread.

There used to be one lady in my usual *paneficio* that always recognized me and gave me a big hello when I walked in. After I'd been going there for a few months, she once commented out of the blue that my Italian was getting better. That was definitely a bit of a boost at the time. I think the key thing was that I had learned the names of the kind of bread we get, which is no small feat, as the labels are never necessarily in the right places by the breads.

Anyway, she retired last year, so now I just say a hello to all the remaining clerks, but it's not quite the same.

Mission accomplished and pretzels purchased! Now we'll turn right out of the *paneficio* and continue down this street, which is called Via Museo. It's another big shopping street here in Bolzano. The architecture is typically Tyrolean, with turrets and towers and cute dormer windows on the buildings on either side of the street. The architecture is in contrast with the modern neon signs on the clothing and housewares shops that line this street.

There's also a small shop that I go to quite a bit; technically, I think, it's called an electronics shop, but it has an odd mix of small appliances, CD blanks, light bulbs, and radios, and little in the way of electronics. However, crucially, it's the place that I go to buy something that allows us to make "the mayor's water" fizzy. Yes, I know that sounds a bit odd. Let me explain.

Chris and I like to drink sparkling water more than still water, and we drink a lot of it every day.

That's the type of water called *aqua frizzante* in Italian, seltzer or club soda in English. Here in Italy, where people drink lots of bottled water, an option is always given in a restaurant: do you want water "with gas" or "without?" Well, that question sounds better in Italian than it does in English; I hesitate to write in English that we like to drink water "with gas."

Anyway, our tap water here in Bolzano comes from the Alps. We do live in the co-capital of the Alps, after all. So our tap water is pretty tasty ... but of course it doesn't come out of the tap "with gas."

Now, the colloquial term for tap water in Italy translates as "the mayor's water." A couple of years ago, there was a big ad campaign to get people to drink less bottled water in Venice, since the empty bottles were clogging up the Venice canals. The official ad campaign dubbed the tap water in Venice *aqua aeritas*, literally "true water." The mayor of Venice, a philosopher by training, appeared in an ad saying, "even the mayor drinks the mayor's water." Cute — get it? A little play on words there. The city even gave away free carafes and machines you could use to carbonate the water, if you preferred to drink it "with gas."

This story just appealed to me on so many levels: calling tap water *aqua veritas*, giving away stylish carafes to encourage people to drink it at home, having a philosopher as the town mayor. This campaign seemed like such a fun approach to solving the problem of too many plastic bottles in the Venice canals.

The part about the existence of machines used to make carbonated water at home was also intriguing. A machine exists to make fizzy water out of tap water? Nice.

I recalled then that when we had been in Venice last year, we had eaten at a restaurant that actually *only* offered tap water, either straight from the tap, or fizzy made with a carbonating machine. And it was pretty good and fairly fizzy.

So we decided to look into getting a machine to carbonate our tap water at home, since we were buying a lot of bottles every week – they are cheaper here in Italy than in North America, but still, they are heavy to lug home. Essentially, the "fizz-maker" machines use a cartridge of food-grade CO_2, combined with a mechanism for forcing it into a bottle of tap water.

It's the same concept I associate with what you see with the little table-top bottles in the old movies from the 1930s and 1940s, where people make themselves a drink at the home bar, and squirt a little fizzy soda water into the scotch. In one of my favorite movies, *Top Hat*, Fred Astaire even does that in time with the music. I'm not sure I'm going to try *that* at home, though.

Now you may think I have digressed, but no, I wanted to bring up that type of machine because in the U.S. that's the only kind of machine that I saw for sale online. Here in Italy, you can get machines that do a bottle at a time, and the cartridges last for a 100 bottles or so.

Anyway, a while back we bought something called the Happy Frizz machine at this electronics shop here on the Via Museo. It's an Italian-made model from just down the road in the city of Trento. Every few weeks I have to keep going back to the store to get a new cartridge of CO2 fizz-making stuff. Eventually it should save money over buying bottled fizzy water, but like most new-fangled things, it will take a while to recoup our investment.

But we've gotta try these things while we're here. As they say, when in Rome ... or Venice ... or Bolzano. I have to say that here in Bolzano, the tap water from the Alps is definitely tastier than the regular tap water in Venice — their mayor would be better off drinking *our* mayor's water.

Back to our discussion of this street we're currently on, the Via Museo. The name means "museum street." I don't know if there has always been a museum on this street, but at the moment it has a museum that houses the most famous resident in Bolzano: our very own world-famous "Iceman" mummy, Ötzi.

Ötzi lived during the Copper Age, 3300 BC (53 centuries ago), and was found in 1991, in the ice, in the Alps, on the border between Austria and Italy. It was eventually determined that he was found on the Italian side, and that's how he came to live in the South Tyrol Museum of Archeology here in Bolzano.

At the museum, there is a comprehensive exhibit on Ötzi's life that talks about when Ötzi lived (during the Copper Age), what clothes he wore, what food he ate and what tools he used, along with the many theories (ever changing over the years) about how he died. His body was so well preserved when he was found, with all his clothing also in good shape, that it's been possible to learn a lot about his life and times. There's even a full-sized reconstruction of what he might have looked like, which really brings him to life.

If you're so inclined, you can also peek through a window into the cold storage unit and see Ötzi's mummified body on display. A little odd, but intriguing if you like that kind of thing.

However, nowhere in the official exhibit do I recall seeing any mention of the "Curse of Ötzi." Clearly an oversight.

It's an interesting legend, even though unlike the Curse of King Tut, there's no convenient curse inscription on the doorway of a tomb to point to as the source of the curse. As I mentioned, Ötzi was found encased in the ice, hence no tomb, no ominous inscription. But mysterious deaths and mummies always make a good tale, and apparently Ötzi's discovery has given rise to a similar kind of mythology surrounding the deaths of a few of the people associated with him, seven of whom have died young. Or mysteriously. Or both.

Unfortunately, as with the Curse of King Tut, the Curse of Ötzi can be countered by a series of facts that dispel each part of the legend, at least according to a website that debunks the curse.

But, to paraphrase Mark Twain, never let facts get in the way of a good story, that's my motto.

And besides, the website that tries to debunk the Curse of Ötzi concludes that the people who benefit most by the story of the curse are the people at the museum here in Bolzano, since in theory the museum could get more people to visit by publicizing the curse story. The problem with that argument is that none of the material about Ötzi that we've seen here in town — either at the museum itself or otherwise — ever talks about the curse. We only learned of it when Chris happened to see a mention of it in an article that was published last year in an Italian newspaper.

The romantic in me likes the fact that Ötzi has his very own curse. I mean, it may be mere hokum, and the people's deaths might just be coincidental, but isn't it more interesting to think that somehow there's a legend associated with the mummy? The King Tut curse story has been going on for all these years, despite all the attempts to debunk it. Maybe Ötzi will someday be as well known asTut, since he now has his very own curse legend. After all, Ötzi doesn't have any gold death mask or anything like King Tut does, so he's got some catching up to do in the publicity department.

Of course, Ötzi does manage to stay in the news, despite the fact he died more than 5,000 years ago. The latest theory about how he died was in the papers recently. As I said, ever since he was discovered encased in the ice 20 years ago, folks have been debating the facts surrounding his death; to me it seems like the theory changes almost annually.

The first theory about how he died was that he just got sick and/or tripped and fell, dying there on the mountain from exposure, all alone.

Later, somebody noticed that x-rays showed an arrowhead buried in his back. So the theory then became that he was attacked by someone, and the attack was what killed him.

Later still, somebody else thought maybe Ötzi was actually the attacker and was killed by the people he was trying to kill.

So, we have Ötzi the solitary wanderer, Ötzi the unfortunate victim of thieves, and/or Ötzi the ruthless plunder and pillager. All different approaches, but always with one common thread: Ötzi died there on the mountain.

Until now. Meet Ötzi the important chieftain, ceremonially buried high up on the Alpine ridge, far away from the valley where he lived and died. Yes, the new theory is that he didn't actually die on the mountain; he was just buried there later, with all pomp and circumstance due his exalted position.

Hmmm. Wow, that is a new one – he's not usually depicted as a king. But hey, why not? King Ötzi – it's got a nice ring to it.

Like all good theories, researchers on both sides are vigorously debating the facts to fit – or deny – this theory.

My favorite argument offered against believing Ötzi's new status is the position they found his body in, with one of his arms hopelessly askew. Kings normally would be positioned in a far more dignified fashion, or so goes the logic of the disbelievers of the new theory.

If you want to take a closer look at his body to see that for yourself without coming to Bolzano, a research institute at EURAC now has a website with new images —some even in 3D— of Ötzi's mummified body. The images, while a bit ghoulish when you consider it's a naked dead body, are quite interesting if you like learning about mummies.

When they launched this website a couple of years ago, it crashed on the first day. The official explanation was that too many people tried to connect to the site all at once and that the heavy amount of traffic brought the web server down.

But then again ... mysterious sudden "death" of the web server? Hmmm.

Maybe there's something to the Curse of Ötzi after all.

Well, now that we've reached the end of Via Museo and have come to the Talvera River, we'll need to cross over to finish the last bit of our errands before we head home. We don't have far to go, we just need to continue across the Talvera bridge, which is just over there, to get to the dry cleaners.

There is a Washing Expert

I should explain a little something about my name before we get to the dry cleaners. For the last 15+ years I have used "Lee" as my first name professionally, although it's actually my middle name. Even though I'm not working at the moment, I still use it here in Italy – it's just force of habit now to say, "my name is Lee" when someone asks me my name.

However, saying that my name is "Lee" does cause people a certain amount of confusion here in Bolzano. They usually doubt that they heard it right, since there are words in Italian pronounced the same way as my name. The Italian word *li* means "them", the Italian word *lì* with an accented "i" means "there". Both are pronounced like Lee.

Needless to say, neither "them" nor "there" is a common first name here.

My usual approach to help alleviate the confusion is to try to explain that it was my grandmother's name. Her name was originally Pasqualena, an Italian name, but as an adult she shortened it to Lee. However, this information typically doesn't really help people here understand why my name is Lee, but I'm not sure why. It may be that I'm not explaining it properly in Italian, of course. But

I'm guessing it's more because calling someone "there" or "them" is just too strange for a name, so people have a bit of trouble adjusting to the fact that my name doesn't sound like a real name.

Which brings us to my interaction with the friendly dry cleaner guy. He is another one of the people I "sort of know" — I see him regularly, but I don't know him well. But, he's always been super friendly and one day he asked me what my name was.

When I told him my name was Lee, he had that momentarily puzzled look I'd come to recognize. He then repeated my name a time or two to be sure he'd heard it correctly. He's a non-native speaker of Italian, from Pakistan I believe, but he's lived in Italy much longer than I have, and he speaks Italian pretty fluently. So I assumed that he was thinking the usual, "What? Her name is 'them' or 'there'? How odd."

Now, the words for "here" and "there" both have other forms as well. So *qua* can be used instead of *qui* for "here" and *la* can be used instead of *lì* for "there." I hear these alternates quite often in Bolzano.

I guess it should have come as no surprise that someone's mental parsing of my name "Lee" as being the same as the word for "there" in Italian got a little muddled. What the dry cleaner clearly remembered was that my name was the same as the word for "there", but he forgot what the sound of the name really was. So the next time he saw me, he greeted me as "La."

Well, actually, I wasn't sure that he did that the first time – it took several more times until I was certain that it wasn't an accident that he always seemed to be telling me something about "there" when I walk through the door. Really, the context of our interactions initially made it unclear – he could have been telling me where to put my clothes on the counter, for example.

But no, after more than a year, I am convinced he thinks my name is "La".

So now, what do I do? Do I try to correct him, or just let it go? After all, he actually tried to remember my name, coming up with something that clearly indicated he processed the original sound of the name properly enough to create a mnemonic aide for it. That's pretty good, I think – I mean, I only see him at most once a week, usually less. So for him to make the effort to remember my name at all I think is impressive. I will confess that I'm lousy at remembering names when I meet someone casually, so I am always impressed when others can remember my name after hearing it just one time. Not surprisingly, but most unfortunately, I promptly forgot his name as soon as I learned it a while back, even though I did want to remember it.

And, since it wasn't clear the first time he called me "La" that he actually thought "La" was my name, it would seem a bit odd to bring it up now, eh?

What would you have done? Try to explain it? Or just let it go? It doesn't bother me that he calls me "La", so is it bad if I just let it go? It just seems like the thing to do, right?

When you hear him call out a cheerful "Ciao, La!" as we enter the dry cleaner's, don't be alarmed. After all, what's in a name?

OK, now that we've picked up the dry cleaning, we're finally done our errands this morning. The fishmonger I like to go to is also in this part of town, but I've decided not to buy any fish today; I think we'll try to go out for dinner, maybe to that Sardinian restaurant if there's a table available.

So it's time to head for home. We'll take this little shortcut through the buildings up to the Talvera River path, so we can use a little wooden pedestrian bridge to cross the river and from there go back along a street that leads to our apartment. On the bridge, make sure you stay to the right – the bridge has lanes for both walkers and bikers, and the bikers whiz by pretty fast, so you don't want to wander over into their lanes. I'm amazed that more people don't get hit by bikes around here – the drivers, I mean the bike drivers, are insane. Oh well, knock wood and *tocca ferro* (which is the Italian version of that saying, literally, "knock metal"), pedestrians don't seem to have a problem dodging the wild bike riders.

Using that route will take us by the only laundromat I know of in town. Have I ever mentioned that earlier this year I decided to declare myself the official "Local Laundromat Pro" this year?

You see, usually I do laundry in our own washing machine, hanging it up to dry since we, like most Italians, have no electric dryer. However, in winter, "hanging it up to dry" means hanging it up inside the apartment. And when you're faced with a pile of sheets and towels, the choice is draping your entire apartment in wet laundry or heading to the laundromat and hoping you can get there early enough to snag the large washer and the dryer before it gets too busy.

Back in March, even though it had been a while since my last visit, I somehow managed to get all the buttons pressed in the right order on the money-taking machine on the wall, even managing to use the discount card I had purchased at one point. Which actually saved me a little money, rather than losing any money by pressing the buttons in the wrong order. Score one for the foreigner.

It was fairly quiet at the laundromat that day, except for one brief moment of activity when several people all trooped in at once, just as I needed to put money in the machine to activate my dryer. This was a key moment for me, actually, as there's a three-minute time limit on putting in the money (in the wall) and getting the dryer started (by pressing the controls on the dryer) before you lose the money. And of course, everyone started asking me questions about the machines all at once.

But handling all that with aplomb and without losing any money is not why I have given myself the Local Laundromat Pro title. You see, in the past, it was only the tourists, the people who didn't speak Italian or German — and therefore the people who couldn't read the signs and controls on the machines— who asked me for advice about the machines and how to use them.

But the family that came in on this day was clearly Italian. There were three people in the group: an adult daughter, her mother, and the daughter's baby in a fancy stroller that took up 1/4 of the length of the laundromat space. What marked them as Italian was how they were dressed: fur-trimmed coats, dresses, and impeccable makeup on the mother and daughter, with the daughter also in heels.

This is not how I, an American residing in Bolzano, or how any tourist I've ever seen, dresses for a laundromat. People here dress up to do everything, though, including going to the supermarket, fruit market, etc. I tend to try to look a bit nicer than the ratty sweats I would have worn years ago to a laundromat, but I can't ever quite get up to the local *fashionista* standards, no matter how hard I try.

Anyway, not only was this family Italian – they were locals. How did I know? They were there to wash a massive knotted cotton throw rug. It was very, very big and it was bright, bright yellow. The daughter asked me – in Italian – for advice on how to wash it.

Now I'm sure since you know me well, you will find this as extremely amusing as I did. What I don't know about the finer points of washing stuff would probably fill a book.

In any case, I made a suggestion of using the larger-size washer, which was available, since I had been using it and, of course, I had just transferred everything to the dryer when these folks walked in. The daughter didn't take my advice at first, but when the rug didn't fit in the smaller washers, she conceded that it needed to go in the big one. Then, like all other first-timers there, she had to figure out where to put the money. It's not obvious, since it goes in a machine on a wall, not in the washing machine itself. So she asked me for help with that, too – the resident expert to the rescue once again.

The name for the laundromat in Italian is *Lava e asciuga* which literally just means "wash and dry." After the rug was in the washer, the daughter then asked if that same machine did both the *lava* (wash) and the *asciuga* (dry) part, or just the washing part. Which was interesting – this woman clearly had never been to a laundromat of any type before. Also, since people here don't have electric clothes dryers at home, I guess it was a reasonable question to ask if a single machine did the washing and the drying. I mean, if you don't have any experience with a dryer, how would you know it's a separate machine, eh?

I explained the dryer vs. the washer functionality, and added that I really thought the rug would do better hanging outside to dry. Well, that's what I would have done with a rug like that – I'd figure it would get all misshapen in a dryer. She seemed skeptical, but in the end decided to go with my advice about that, too.

When you're a Local Laundromat Pro, you offer all kinds of advice, at no extra charge.

The family left the laundromat while their washing machine was running, and came back with five minutes to go in their cycle. Which was just about the time I was taking my sheets out of the dryer and folding them to put into the rolling suitcase I use as a going-to-the-laundromat laundry basket. Seeing me, the mother/grandmother, in her fur-trimmed coat and fancy skirt, put down her purse, smiled at me, picked up one end of the sheet I was currently folding and then proceeded to help me fold the sheet. And then picked up the next sheet and helped me fold that one, too, and then the next one, and the next one.

While this was happening, her daughter started announcing the time remaining on their wash cycle: "four minutes, Mama" ..."three minutes, Mama."

At that moment, I felt like we'd entered into some type of sporting event, where there's a time limit, and the announcer is calling off the laps or periods remaining to get to the finish line. For whatever reason, the daughter wasn't happy about her mother helping the local laundromat pro fold her sheets as they waited; she would have preferred her to focus on watching their laundry spin in their machine during the final minutes.

Her mother and I finished folding the last sheet just as the daughter announced in an agitated way "one minute, Mama." Not to be rushed, her mother got a couple of pillowcases folded, too, before their rug came out of the washer.

So it was a meeting between the Local Laundromat Pro and the extremely friendly and gracious Local Folding Pro. We could be quite a team at the next Laundry Olympics.

Of course, having a washing machine inside the apartment doesn't necessarily mean smooth sailing with the laundry. Indeed, the original washer that came with our apartment figured prominently on one memorable day.

It had all started well as I set out on my usual everyday expeditions. I decided to stop at the local *Acqua & Sapone* store (literally the name just means Water and Soap), which is kind of like a North American Walgreens or CVS store, only without all the drugs, and on a much smaller scale. It's where I'd been buying our soap, and as we'd just opened the last pack, I thought I'd stop and get some more.

So I'm waiting at the counter behind a woman who is buying a pair of sunglasses. There's a speck of dirt or something that she wants the cashier to clean off before she buys them. This drags on for about five minutes.

Finally, that's finished, and the woman's many purchases – including the now clean sunglasses – are bagged up by the cashier and set off to the side on the counter, per the usual routine at this store. The cashier then turns away from the woman, who's still standing at the counter doing something, and rings up my soap.

Now, to give you an idea, this is a very small checkout area, so I'm in front of the cashier to give her the money, but still next to me, on my right, is the woman with the sunglasses, fiddling with her purse. She is therefore still in front of the end of the counter to my right. So in front of her is the area where her bag is, which is generally the area where the cashier puts the bagged items for you to pick up after you pay.

As I get my money out, I notice the cashier has put the soap into a bag for me, but then I lose track of the bag while I'm paying. The cashier hands me my receipt and turns to the next customer. I turn to the right where I expect that the cashier has put my bag … but it's not there. I ask the cashier, where's my bag? And she gestures toward the empty space to my right and then also notices that there's no bag to be seen.

What clearly must have happened is that the woman with the sunglasses picked up my bag along with hers – it's the logical explanation, since she was still puttering around there while I was getting my money out, although she left while I was putting my wallet away.

Now, the question is, who's responsibility is it to make sure

I got my bag in the first place? I say the cashier, since I never actually had the bag – heck, I barely saw the bag, I was too busy getting my money out. And the cashier put my bag down next to/along side of the other woman's bag(s). However, the cashier says it's my responsibility and not her problem. Since I took the receipt for the purchase, so her argument goes, her part was done. And too bad if I don't have my bag. Hmph.

The manager comes over, and I explain it to her, and she says, after agreeing with the cashier, that the best solution is for me go get the stuff back from the woman with the sunglasses. Well, interesting idea, but of course, I don't know that woman and neither do they. So their next suggestion is to wait for the lady to bring the stuff back and check back with them in a day or two.

Now, this sunglass buyer was pretty high maintenance, in my humble opinion. I mean, I waited five minutes while she went through a long back-and-forth about the spot on the sunglasses. What are the odds she is going to bother to go back to the store to bring back a little bag of soap?

Anyway, this debate goes on for a while – I don't have all the right vocabulary looked up in advance for this kind of situation, but I'm trying to say that I just want replacement soap, or the money back. I mean, it wasn't a deliberate malicious act on the part of the cashier or the sunglasses woman or anything, but I was busy paying for the stuff when it disappeared, and it seems like I should not have to pay for nothing, right? So essentially, my argument is that the cashier should not have put the bag down along with the woman's bag where she could so easily take it, and since I never had the bag, it wasn't my fault that I don't have the soap now, and I should not have to pay for something I don't have. But the manager says no, there's nothing to be done, but if I want, I can report the "theft" of the soap to the police. And she proceeds to call the police.

Ah, my day is getting better and better, clearly.

Anyway, I call Chris to get the vocabulary so I can make it clear to the police that I just think it was an honest mistake on the part of the cashier to put my bag with the other woman's bag, but that it wasn't my fault the bag wasn't given to me, so that's why I want more soap or the money back. Since, after all, I have paid the store for things I never received.

However, when the police arrive, after they look at my passport, and then at the manager's identity card, they explain to me that because I accepted the receipt for the purchase, it's no longer the store's problem. Which had been the position of the cashier from the beginning, of course.

Interesting, since the system here, in my experience, is that you always get/take the receipt before you pick up your purchase. So in theory, a store could have an intentional scam not to give you the merchandise, and if you accepted the receipt, you'd be stuck. That's not what happened here, but still...

However, I don't say any of that to the police, of course. The cops are puzzled as to why the heck they have been brought in on this in the first place? Did I buy an expensive bottle of perfume or something? No? Only a package of soap? They find it odd that someone called them, and explain that I can't file a theft report on something so small. (Of course, I never wanted to file the report in the first place; that was all the manager's idea).

Anyway, one of the cops tells me to leave my phone number with the store, and then if the woman comes back with the soap, the store should call me to come get it.

Vabbè! as they say here – essentially "OK, fine, whatever."

I felt somewhat vindicated later that I wasn't totally out-of-line with the culture here when I told locals we know about what had happened. They all agreed with me that the store's position wasn't right, and that the store should have made good on the purchase by just giving me a replacement bar of soap and letting it go at that. People also thought it was very odd that the manager called the police in for this, and also odd that in general I was told that my accepting the receipt was enough to make the soap "my" soap, even if I never actually got the bag with the soap after I paid.

BTW, it wasn't that it was a lot of money for the soap, it was just the initial surprise of what the heck happened to the bag of soap that spurred me to make such an issue of this. Later, it was the unexpected position that the store took that was at first surprising, and then just a little annoying and odd, that kept me pressing for my soap.

Anyway, that would have been plenty of excitement for one morning, but as I was on my way back to the apartment a little while later, Gemma, a friend in our building, called me on my cell phone to tell me water was seeping out from under our apartment door into the hallway.

Aack.

I'd left a load of laundry finishing in the washing machine when I left, and the water had exploded all over the place by the time I arrived home. Fortunately, the bathroom and hallway floors in the apartment were the only place the water went within the apartment, and both are linoleum tile, not carpet. And our apartment hallway apparently slants downward toward the apartment door, so much of the water was collected in a pool by the front door both inside our apartment and also out in the hall and down the stairs outside our apartment as well. What a mess.

I guess the apartment floors were due for a mopping, so I suppose it could have been much worse. Still, I did wonder how you say that English lyric "Mamma said there'd be days like this" in Italian. For days like this.

As it turned out, later that night a woman called from *Acqua & Sapone* to tell me to come pick up my soap. There was a long explanation that I didn't quite follow on the phone: either the woman with the sunglasses brought it back, or they decided just to replace the soap, since making me talk to the police over the disappearance of something worth three euros was kind of ridiculous. I went back the next day and picked up the soap. The new (to me) cashier had clearly been warned to expect me, and she just gave me a bag with the soap without saying a word. The manager and other cashier were nowhere in sight. So in the end, I got no apology or anything else to give me real satisfaction about the resolution. All I got was all I ever wanted to begin with: the soap.

Vabbè.

———————————————————

A Place to call Home

Now that we've finally finished all our errands we've come back to the apartment to unload our purchases and start on lunch – Chris will be back from his office on his lunch break by 12:30. That's one fun thing about living in Italy: most people here still go home for lunch. Chris can take up to two hours for his lunch break; for some folks in Italy it's traditionally a three-hour midday break. It was interesting when I was talking to one of our neighbors at some point and realized that she was asking me what time Chris would be home for lunch. It was a question solely about the time he arrived – it was not a question of whether he came home for lunch. That's just expected .

Anyway, you probably noticed as we arrived at our building that we live pretty close to the city center. We live in this older apartment complex designed by a semi-famous architect in the 1920s.

It's painted yellow, with ornately carved white decorations on the sides of the buildings. The complex has seven buildings, four floors each, and each building has a terrace on the roof. We happened to luck into finding a rental unit in this place; we rent from the daughter of the (now deceased) previous owner.

This building's style is unique in our neighborhood. The complex was originally built for the Italian government workers who were being resettled in Bolzano from other parts of Italy in the 1920s, right after Mussolini took over.

However, at some point, Mussolini decided he didn't really like this kind of ornate architecture. All through town you can find the resulting buildings built in the 1920s and 1930s in the Mussolini preferred, boxy Fascist style. Unfortunately, the architect of our building didn't do designs in that style, so he fell out of favor and didn't get any more government building commissions after that.

I'd actually noticed this building while walking through town one day, and thought it really looked like a building that was in Europe, rather than some of the newer apartment buildings here which don't have much to distinguish them from buildings in Vancouver, where we used to live. So, I'm happy that we're living in something that actually seems more European than North American.

———————————————————

Life in a cute, older apartment building isn't without its own set of complications, not all of which are charming. For example, before we could actually move into our apartment, we had our first challenge: unlocking the apartment doors. Our apartment has two doors, side by side, that both have locks. On the door on the left-side, there's one keyhole. On the door on the right-side there are two keyholes, one above the other. If you view them as a logic puzzle to be solved, you're in good shape. If you're expecting just to be able to get into the apartment on the first try, you will be sadly mistaken.

We had decided to stop by the apartment the evening we picked up the keys. Although our lease technically didn't start until the following day, the landlady had said we should feel free to go in early, so we figured what the heck.

From a problem our estate agent had with the keys when she tried to show the apartment to us the first time, we knew that the bottom keyhole on the right-side door did not work and there was no key for it, so we were supposed to just ignore that.

OK, good, that left two locks to deal with, one on the left-side door, and one on the right-side door. It was simple to figure out which key went in which lock - the two keys are quite distinct. We had been told that the left-side door's lock was odd, and that you turned it in "the unexpected direction" to lock and unlock the lock on that side.

Ah, yes. "The unexpected direction." And which direction would that be? Not being sure, we put the key in on the left-side door, and it turned in one direction. And turned. And turned some more. Hmm - was this right, or were we doing something wrong? Were we turning it the wrong way? The right way? The "unexpected direction" way? There was no way to tell.

Then we tried the lock on the right-side door; that key seemed to turn once to the right, but then we couldn't get it to turn again in any direction.

Argh and double argh.

Hot — it was the middle of summer and summers are hot and humid in Bolzano — sweaty, tired and more than a little frustrated and discouraged, we decided that the problem must be that the sole set of keys I had carried with me in my purse was defective. We had actually received four sets, but I hadn't thought to bring more than one, since they looked identical. So, we wound up leaving without actually getting into the apartment that night.

First thing the next morning, armed with all the sets of keys, we set about to tackle the door again. Remember how I said it was a logic puzzle? We finally got the doors open by my turning the key in the lock on the left, one turn at a time, and Chris then turning the key in the lock on the right each time, to see if it would open. Trial and error, and a lot of patience, and finally the doors opened.

And then we spent another 10 minutes figuring out how to *lock* the doors again properly. When we finally got it figured out, it turned out not to be as hard as it seemed. But that's only true once you know which direction to turn the key in the left-side lock (it turns to the right), and you have to know that you have to turn it *six times* before the lock is fully disengaged.

That's not a typo: six turns of that key is required for the lock on the left.

The right-side door lock has a special spring in it, which needs to be engaged in order to turn it. Not hard, if you know that's what you're looking for, but none of this was obvious on our first try.

On that swelteringly hot and humid summer morning, when we finally made it into the apartment, we were rewarded with a nice blast of cool air. While there's no air conditioning, the apartment building was built back in the 1920s, and the thick walls keep the hot air on the outside and the cooler air on the inside in summer. They sure knew how to build them back then.

Yes, it's quite a charming place to live, once you figure out how to get in.

Of course that initial struggle getting into the apartment wasn't our only adventure with the locks.

Nope, we later had a bit of a flashback to that day when we arrived home and couldn't open the door.

Just to review: we have these two locks on the apartment doors, with two different keys, on the two side-by-side doors:

Lock #1 is a fancy security-type thing that locks automatically when you close the door. It requires at least a half-turn with the key to get the door open. To completely lock this one after you leave, you turn the key twice to fully engage all the mechanisms.

Lock #2 is a big security bar, and it requires six turns of the key to lock it from the outside. It does not automatically lock when you close the door, you have to use the key to lock that door. Because of the loud noise it makes when you go to lock it, everyone in the building knows when we're coming and going. One of our neighbors once told me she knew we must be away at one point as she hadn't heard the locks in a couple of days.

Anyway, we'd gone out for some errands on a Saturday morning and decided to drop off our purchases at the apartment at about 11:45 a.m., before heading back out for lunch at a local restaurant. We got to the apartment and unlocked lock #2 per usual - the strategy is to unlock lock #2 first, and then lock #1, since the final half-turn of lock #1 allows the door to swing open.

We'd done this hundreds of times by now. But when the key went into lock #1 that Saturday morning, it wouldn't turn.

This had happened once or twice to me in the past, usually when I'd had the shopping cart full of groceries. I told Chris, no problem, just jiggle the door a little and then it will work. But 10 minutes later, after we've both tried multiple times, it's definitely not working.

OK, this was annoying, but not a huge problem, since we didn't have anything that had to go into the refrigerator. So, now, it was just a matter of calling our landlady and/or her handyman and have one of them come deal with it.

Except... I suddenly realized that my cell phone with their phone numbers on it was not in my bag. I'd apparently forgotten to take it with me that morning, so it was sitting safely in the apartment. Where we couldn't get to it, of course, since we couldn't get into the apartment.

Chris had his cell phone, but we'd never put those numbers in his cell phone, since I'd always been the one to contact the landlady and handyman.

Aack.

Now, what to do? It did not occur to me to try to look the phone numbers up in a phone book, as a) I hadn't ever tried finding someone in a paper phone book here and b) I didn't know where either of them actually lived and which phone book they would be listed in and c) I wasn't sure where I'd go to find a phone book in any case. The only one I knew of was in our apartment, on a table not far from my cell phone.

So, while we knew we needed a locksmith, the question was how to find one. The people we knew in the building weren't around, so asking them was out.

Then it occurred to me that maybe the local tobacconist would know the name of a locksmith. The tobacconist has a shop down the block from our apartment. I should explain that a "tobacconist" shop in Italy seems to have a little of everything - kind of like a 7-11, without the food except for candies, but with batteries and tissues and newspapers and lottery tickets and gum and a whole host of other odds and ends. The owner of the one down the street is another one of those people I "sort of know," who recognizes me when I stop by. Our interactions are pretty brief: I say hi, he says hi, I hand over my one-euro coin for the paper, and we're done. He also will occasionally save the English inserts in the International Herald Tribune for me, remembering that I had originally been buying that English-language paper when we first arrived. Now I buy the local Italian-language paper instead, since Chris likes to read that occasionally.

Anyway, I'm not sure if I really expected the tobacconist to be prepared for this kind of question, but since his shop was only a block away, it seemed like a place to start.

So, I headed over to his shop, thinking, OK, I know the vocabulary for sentences like "there is a problem with our apartment door" and "the door does not open with this key." I crucially don't know the word for "lock," but decide to wing it anyway. So, at the tobacconist shop, I use all the vocabulary I can think of, pantomiming the act of turning a key in the lock while saying in Italian something like "there is a problem, our apartment door, the key doesn't open it." All said while using my key as a prop, of course.

The tobacconist nods calmly and says in Italian, "ah, yes, the key doesn't open the door" (or words to that effect). He then pulls out a small notebook, page after page covered with lists of handwritten telephone numbers. He flips through it and finds the number for a locksmith who is nearby. He writes down the phone number and mentions that the guy works on Saturdays. Perfect.

After thanking the tobacconist profusely, I head off back to the apartment door, where Chris has been valiantly still trying the key (to no avail). He calls the number. We then spend 45 minutes waiting outside the building until help is finally at hand: the locksmith shows up and within a minute he's used a little tool to unlock the door.

Idle thought: if a general tool exists that can so easily open a fancy lock like that, what is the point of having special keys for the lock in the first place?

In any case, the locksmith tries this, that, and the other thing once the door is open, and then declares lock #1 to be broken and unable to be unlocked with a key anymore, and unable to be fixed - it will need to be replaced.

You may recall that a feature of lock #1 is that it automatically locks the door when you close the door. As it turned out, *that _ part of this lock still worked, so the locksmith had to disable that part, so that door no longer locked when you closed the door, since otherwise we wouldn't have been able to unlock it. A perfect example of when a feature is not a necessarily _desirable* feature at all times.

In the end, we were left with a disabled lock #1 and a perfectly functional lock #2 with all of its six key-turns. So, we could then get in and out of the apartment and lock it up when we left, which was about all that could be done on a Saturday. All in all, a basically happy (if expensive) ending, finished in time for a late lunch at the restaurant.

People often ask me about comparative prices of things

between here and North America. For the record, an emergency locksmith visit on a Saturday is just as expensive here as it would be in North America.

We can look, however, at the overall positives of the experience, I suppose. At least it ...wasn't raining ...wasn't snowing ...wasn't a Sunday ...wasn't late at night ... didn't happen when we were coming back with perishables ... didn't happen when we were coming back tired from a trip.

And now we know that the tobacconist is the font of all information — or at least he has a whole notebook of numbers for emergencies. Hopefully, we'll never have occasion to find out what those other numbers are for.

Anyway, now what we've unlocked the doors, welcome to our apartment! It came fully furnished, including pots, pans, dishes, lamps, and furniture in every room – we even have a dining room set that seats eight for all those dinner parties we never give. Chris nicknamed the guest room/spare bedroom "the cell," since it's very small, and with just a single bed, desk, and small wardrobe cabinet, it seems very basic and austere. I'll give you a grand tour, but first follow me into the kitchen so I can put away the groceries.

By the way, even though it's polite here to pause at the doorway and ask permission before entering a room in someone's house or apartment, you don't need stand on ceremony with me when we get to the kitchen. The idea is that when you are at the entrance to a room, you say, *Permesso?* which means, essentially, "Do I have your permission to come in to the room now?"

Hearing this always brings to my mind the custom in British royal courts – or at least the custom as shown in those BBC series set in royal courts – where you have to ask "permission to withdraw" before leaving the presence of the king. But here it's not just with royalty that this applies – it's with everyone, and it's permission to get *into* the room that's the issue. It's the custom to ask it when you are about to enter every single room of a house, not just the first room you come to.

So, when I take you on a tour of the whole apartment, to be well mannered according to the customs here, you would really need to pause and ask *Permesso?* at the doorway of each room before following me into the room. At least this is the generalization of the behavior that Chris and I have observed our Italian friends doing when they visit us.

The tricky bit is that since this is not at all like what we'd do in the U.S. or Canada, it's harder than you'd think to remember this once you're inside someone's apartment. In the U.S., once someone invites you in and is taking you on a tour of their apartment, you're pretty much good to go anywhere in the apartment with them.

So, when Chris and I remember to do this at all, we typically do it at the front door only, although we'd like to be able to do it properly for the other rooms if that's what we're supposed to do. When we're visiting someone together, Chris and I both try to be on the alert and hope that one of us remembers to say it when we go from room to room, which works about 50% of the time. Personally, I just don't have an intuition for when I need to do it; in fact, I even feel kind of awkward pausing in the doorway when the person I'm following is already halfway across into the next room. I'd like to do the polite thing; I'm just not clear on all the rules and how it really works. Hopefully, in the same way my bad grammar is excused by only having learned how to speak some Italian a short time ago, any accidental impolite behavior can also be overlooked.

———————————————————————————

This rule applies to anyone who goes into an apartment, by the way, including repair people. I've been struck by how our handyman who comes to fix things always used to ask "*Permesso?*" to enter each room when he'd come. Since he was there because I'd asked him to come by in order to fix something in a particular room, from my North American perspective it seemed like my original invitation should have automatically given him leave to enter the room in question. I noticed the last time he came, though, he only said "*Permesso?*"at the front door. Maybe there's an automatic exception after you've visited a place X number of times, or something. That's the problem with the rules you don't know — they may cover all kind of contingencies, it's just hard to figure them out without a playbook.

It was actually quite funny when this happened with a different handyman once, who had come to fix a problem with one of our windows. He asked "*Permesso?*" at the front door and "*Permesso?*" at the door to the second bedroom (where the problem window was). Every time he came to find me in the living room, he stayed at the doorway without entering the room — because he hadn't asked "*Permesso?*" for that room, I guess.

When he asked if I had a ladder, I tried to take him to it so he could carry it himself back to the room where he was working. We have a huge ladder that came with the apartment – to say it's taller than I am doesn't really convey just how big this ladder is, of course, given my relative lack of height. Let's just say the doorways in the apartment are at least seven-feet tall, and the ladder is taller than that.

Anyway, it's stored behind the door in the master bedroom, which meant it needed to be maneuvered through that doorway, the apartment hallway, and then through the doorway into the second bedroom. The repairman of course stopped in the doorway of the master bedroom, not following me into the room. However, I didn't really want to have to fuss with the huge, heavy ladder by myself if I didn't have to, so I tried to grant him leave to enter the room after me — without him having asked, "*Permesso?*" I repeated my "it's OK, you can come in here" phrase several times before he finally consented to crossing the bedroom's threshold to get the ladder.

Maybe there's something in the rules that doesn't allow permission to be granted if it hasn't been asked for? Or maybe it has to do with general restrictions on going into a master bedroom? Or maybe I don't know the right phrase for granting proper permission and so it didn't sound official enough?

Or maybe he just didn't want to have to carry that large, awkward, heavy ladder either.

Now, when he couldn't fix the window on the first visit, he just left the ladder in the second bedroom. So, there was no need to go through the whole "*Permesso*?" thing again with the ladder when he came back the next day.

However, at some point that second day he again came to find me in the living room, hovering in the doorway as before. He then posed a more complicated question than the previous day's question about the ladder. I didn't quite follow it, so I went out into the hallway where he was and asked him repeat the question.

What I heard was "something something something – need to go to my car – something something something – key."

Hmm. I often get pieces of sentences like this, but I typically understand a bit more than 50% of the words these days. In situations like this, though, I try to make my best guess as to what he could be saying. What would you have guessed?

My first thought was maybe he wanted to borrow my keys so that he didn't need to ring the bell when he came back from going out to his car for something.

But no, that wasn't it; he shook his head and repeated his question.

I still only caught "something something something – need to go to my car – something something something – key". I didn't really understand it any better when I heard it the second time.

But I was game – I tried again to guesstimate what he needed. So, my second try was maybe he needs to bring his car into the courtyard for something; workmen occasionally do this, and it requires using a special key to unlock the courtyard gate so it can be swung open wide enough for a car.

Or, I thought, maybe he needed to drive into the building complex parking lot in the first place, which requires an electronic gate opener. So I offered him both of those "keys."

Which got me only another, more adamant, shaking of his head. My saying in Italian, "I'm sorry but I didn't understand your question," was probably completely unnecessary at that point, but it was the best I could come up with, since I was stumped and out of guesses.

In desperation, he went back into the second bedroom, rummaged around in his bag, pulled out a screwdriver, and then said what I took to be "no, what I'm trying to tell you is that I need a non Phillips-head kind of screwdriver, which

I have in my car; I have only this Phillips-head kind in my bag. Do you happen to have one here to save me the trip to my car?"

Well, that's what I understood from the interaction. I think what he actually said was something more like "I need a different one of these" while pointing to the screwdriver in his hand. Short, but simple and to the point. And, really, much easier for me to follow with the visual aid to see that the "key" I thought he was talking about was really a screwdriver.

Now, in my own defense I would like to point out the following: I did correctly recognize that he was saying something about going to his car, and none of my Italian conversation tapes had ever covered the word for screwdriver. Plus, the Italian word for "key" is *chiave* [key-ah-vay]; the word for screwdriver is *cacciavite* [kah-chah-vee-tay]. Close. OK, so maybe not *that* close. But when you don't recognize the word for screwdriver and are trying to figure out a word that might have something to do with a car, I would argue that it's a reasonable interpretation.

Well, that's my story and I'm sticking to it.

And, yes, I did have the right kind of screwdriver, so we were finally in business. And off he went to fix the window.

Now this poor guy had originally tried to get my landlady to be our go-between when he came to the apartment, since he knew I didn't speak much Italian, and he didn't speak English. However, she didn't have time and told him I spoke

Italian well enough.

Well, yes and no, apparently.

Anyway, here we are in the kitchen; you might have noted that we don't have all the modern appliances we had in our last few houses. We have a gas stove, but no microwave. There's our "Happy Frizz" machine, of course, but no toaster, no blender and no garbage disposal in the sink.

We do have a little refrigerator tucked under the counter – it's so small you might not have noticed it at first. It's the newer version of the really old one that came with our apartment. But even though it's new it has retained some of the original's old-world charm: it's a non frost-free refrigerator.

Did you know that "frost-free" is a bit of a misnomer, actually? All refrigerators allow frost to build up; the "frost-free" ones automatically get rid of the frost for you, while the old style ones allow you the thrill of doing that yourself. While they do have "frost-free" refrigerators in Italy, our apartment came with very old appliances, and our first refrigerator was not one of those new-fangled modern types. Nope, not by a long shot. So every couple of months, I had the pleasure of defrosting the refrigerator.

And it is a pleasure, not work, of course. How else can you describe:

- The hours of gently melting the ice with boiled water and steam
- The opportunities to chop daintily at the stubbornly not-melting bits with a knife, using skill and strategy to avoid hitting a freezer coil
- The lovely cold-water puddles that afford the chance to wash the kitchen floor, over and over
- The feeling of quiet satisfaction when a mosquito – who is either the one who had the midnight snack on your arm last night or her close cousin – dive bombs toward you, only to miss and wind up drowning in the pan of water beside you
- The victorious moment when you hear the "ka-thunk" that signals that the last chunk of ice, previously stranded just out of reach in the back above the freezer compartment, has finally landed on the refrigerator floor, sounding an end to the day's defrosting festivities.

Our original refrigerator was on its last legs even when we moved in; it eventually didn't seem to keep things as cold as it once did, and the handle threatened daily to come off. Finally, our landlady promised to buy us a new one, which is what we have now.

However, we realized even before we got it that there would be a better-than-even chance that our new refrigerator would also be a non frost-free one, since the small ones that fit into our kitchen space usually don't have the frost-free feature.

Of course, the ones that have to be defrosted manually are supposedly more energy efficient, too, a fact I always considered with great appreciation each time I saw how the ice had inexorably built up around the otherwise pretty ineffectual freezer compartment.

So, even with the new refrigerator — which is indeed not a frost-free one —my defrosting opportunities continue. I count myself quite fortunate in that regard, since I hadn't had a chance to do this kind of thing for many years, I think going all the way back to when I was in college. There's nothing like defrosting to bring back those carefree college days, as well as providing a reminder of the all the unanticipated charms of living in an old apartment in Europe.

Now, it's possible that I *might* be willing to give up *some* of the fun while you're here. Make me an offer. I warn you, though, it's going to cost you, since I won't easily relinquish such a meditative, relaxing, fun-filled way to spend an afternoon.

After all, and with apologies to Mark Twain, it's not every day that a woman gets to defrost a refrigerator.

Language Lessons

Living in this building has actually helped with my efforts to learn Italian in several ways. Learning Italian was one of my original goals, along with learning how to do grocery shopping, laundry, and paperwork in Italy. I could write a whole book on that last topic alone — paperwork here truly is a never-ending journey.

Actually, come into the living room, and I'll tell you one quick paperwork story. Notice anything missing in here that you might have expected to see? Yes, it's true — we don't have a TV. Take a seat there on one of our two cute, but unfortunately rather uncomfortable, little red sofas while I tell you about doing the "TV Tax Tandem."

I gave it that name as an ironic reference to the language "tandems" I use to practice my Italian, where I meet with a native speaker of Italian, and we swap Italian for English conversational practice. However, dealing with the RAI (the Italian TV company) office was only accidentally a sort of series of tandem sessions, in that I got to practice my Italian and even learned some new vocabulary during my adventures. There was no possibility of doing it in English, of course – all Italian, all the time. Well, except for a little of the part that involved my landlady — but wait, I'm getting ahead of myself.

In Italy there is a yearly TV tax that is assessed by the

state TV company, RAI. The bill arrives in January, and you pay ahead for the coming year. This tax is assessed on every television that you have in your house – and you are required to register every set with the state.

Not paying the tax is actually a quite common approach among locals, as it turns out. But when you're a stranger in a land of strange taxes, you tend to want to be honest about these kinds of things, just in case. So last year we paid the tax, since our landlady had put the TV in our name, since our apartment came with a TV. Figuring out how and where to pay the 2009 tax was a saga in our first year, but in the end, it all worked out.

In October 2009, though, the TV system in Italy switched over to the digital system, just like it did in the U.S. Older TVs don't work with the new system — you need a new TV or a converter box, or something.

Now, Chris and I actually rarely watch TV, even when we're living in a country where the programs are broadcast in a language we both can follow. Here in Italy, the number of times we watched the TV in our apartment could be counted on one hand and still have fingers left over. I had thought at one point I might check out the Italian re-runs of the old 1970s _Starsky and Hutch _TV series that debuted with much fanfare on Italian TV shortly after we arrived in Bolzano. Watching TV is supposed to be a good way to learn a language, they say. But I never did get around to trying that. So we didn't really need to have a TV in our apartment.

When we got the TV tax bill this year, I contacted our landlady to ask her what she was going to do about the TV, since it didn't work anymore with the new system. Since the bill was in Chris's name, my suggestion was that we would put the TV back in her name, and then she could do whatever she wanted with the TV.

So off I went to the RAI office to find the form to change the TV registration from Chris' name to our landlady's name (Ms. B). I went armed with our lease, to show that Ms. B was our landlady, and that both Chris' name and my name were associated with the apartment. This was critical, since the bill was only in his name, not in my name, but the RAI office was only open during Chris's work hours, so there was no way for him to go there. Chris and I don't have the same last name, since I didn't change my name when we got married. In the U.S. that is occasionally a problem, since few women there keep their maiden names these days. Interestingly, though, here in Italy it is the norm for married women to keep their maiden names. So, having two different last names and getting people to believe we are married is never a problem here. At least there's one aspect of paperwork that is easier in Italy, I guess.

OK, so I'm at the RAI office, and I show the woman there our TV tax bill and the apartment lease and explain the whole thing in flawed but hopefully coherent Italian. All for the purpose of changing the TV registration back to Ms. B's name. But, of course, it turns out that while a landlady can change the name of the TV registration to the tenant's name without the tenant's signature, the reverse is not true. Ah, well, I didn't really expect this to work on the first try.

Back home I contact Ms. B to explain the situation. She calls RAI and then calls me – using Italian, which she rarely does with me, since she speaks English very well. So this was part of my extra tandem practice, on the phone, even, chatting about TV taxes and registration forms. All with vocabulary I had just learned that week, too, and using advanced grammar points I had forgotten about like the passive voice for verbs. I.e. the forms get filled out "by someone," they do not fill themselves out.

As a result of our conversation, Ms. B and I agree that she will physically remove the TV from the apartment and then go with me to fill out the form to unregister the TV, since she removed the TV from the apartment. The TV would still be in Chris' name, if an unregistered TV is still in someone's name, but that sounds like an "if a tree falls in the forest" type of question, which I hope is neither here nor there for TVs in Italy.

So, back I go to the RAI office to meet Ms. B.

Oddly, the TV tax is unexpectedly causing me to get extra exercise, since the RAI office is on the other side of town. The concept of a TV ever being the cause of getting extra exercise strikes me as funny, since a TV is supposed to make you a couch potato, and here I am building up some calf muscles with all this back and forth to that office. I lose weight here in Italy when I eat lots of gelato (no, seriously, I really do) and when I deal with TV issues – who would have thought.

At the RAI office, Ms. B offers to fill out the necessary form, which is fine with me, as it's all in Italian. But the form is so convoluted that even she (an Italian) requires an assist from the RAI woman. I don't even want to know what the problems were with the terms on the form. But we inch closer to being done when it turns out that Ms. B has given the TV to a friend.

Whoops, hold the phone. We now have yet more paper-work that suddenly needs to be involved.

Now, it was always going to be the case that Ms. B would need to write a letter that she had removed the TV from the apartment. And it was also always going to be necessary for Chris both to sign a form stating that he had no TV in his apartment and also to provide a copy of his passport to turn in with said form.

But now, with the TV having been given to the friend, we also needed the friend to sign the form to state that she has the TV. And, the friend needed to provide a copy of her Italian identity card to add to the document packet.

Maybe it's just me, but doesn't this start to seem like we were dealing with the provenance of some valuable work of art, not a 15-year-old (or more) TV that doesn't even work without a converter box? It was such an amazing set of bureaucratic requirements that even Ms. B was floored. And none of this was made this complicated because Chris and I are foreigners. It's just complicated, even if you're

Italian.

But fortunately, once we knew what to do, the process, while multi-stepped, time-consuming and cumbersome, was not impossible to complete.

So, having finally assembled all the required signatures, documents, photocopies, etc., I went back over to the RAI office one more time and triumphantly handed the collected paperwork packet to the RAI lady behind the counter. She checked everything, and said I was done and free to go.

But wait. I've lived here long enough and done enough paperwork now that I wanted — nay, needed — a paper in return with some sort of stamp or signature on it. Preferably both. After all, doesn't all paperwork end with that here? Yes, of course it does.

So, in my best, possibly still woefully ungrammatical Italian, I asked for my precious stamped document to take home. Which I got.

Of course, it's a document that I hope I never need, because — with luck — we will never get a TV tax bill here again.

———————————————————————

Now you see that there is a perfectly logical explanation for why we don't have a TV in our apartment. But at least it did provide a rather unusual way to practice my Italian, and that is one of my major ongoing goals.

While I haven't learned Italian as fluently as I would have liked, I have progressed from knowing zero two years ago — I mean, does knowing how to order a cappuccino really count as knowledge of the language, no matter how useful? — to the point where I am now comfortable enough to be able to spend the occasional afternoon chatting almost exclusively in Italian.

So, while I'm not fluent yet, that's progress, right?

As I said, this building has definitely factored into prompting me to develop some skills in Italian conversation. For example, there was my motivation to learn enough to be able to speak with one of our upstairs neighbors, who I bumped into almost every day when we first arrived. She's now 90 years old and climbs up and down four sets of stairs every day when she goes out on *her* daily morning errands.

Although I did learn her real name a long time ago, I will forever think of her as *la signora della scala*, which means "the lady of the stairs," since I would run into her in the stairwell of our building each day.

In fact, before she learned my name, she would actually greet me (in Italian) by exclaiming "Ah, hello, (I see) it's the married lady from the stairwell" – i.e., she would call *me la signora della scala*. Too funny, eh?

Anyway, *la signora della scala* has always been very friendly even though in the beginning our conversations were restricted to simple greetings and the weather; she spoke no English and I spoke little Italian. She would always tell me she wanted me to learn Italian so we could talk, which seemed like a fun idea to me.

So, I would valiantly try to remember more and more vocabulary and grammar each time we met. Unfortunately all that material would go fleeing from my mind while on the spot trying to converse with her. Ah well. But still, we would carry on our limited conversations in those early days, and I would struggle to comprehend as much as I could and hope the next time would be better.

Nowadays when I see her, I realize that I now speak and understand enough Italian to chat with her more confidently. Although I have to admit that there's still always something I don't quite follow in every conversation with her. But, I do detect major progress on that front. We can now talk in more detail about the weather, at least, as well as some other general stuff. But, there's only so much you can fit into a two-minute conversation in the stairwell, I guess.

During one of our early conversations, *la signora dell scala* suggested that speaking Italian with someone regularly would help me learn more quickly. This is essentially the notion of that "tandem language" exchange I mentioned before, which is quite popular here in Bolzano.In a tandem language exchange, two speakers help each other learn their native languages through conversational practice, with one-on-one sessions scheduled one or more times per week.

I actually decided to focus on this kind of learning/practice shortly after we first arrived, partly because the opportunities for the sessions happened to come my way, and partly because I was bored with the class I briefly took the first year. We weren't practicing speaking at all in that class, which was really what I wanted; in theory, I can study grammar on my own, although I will admit that I'm not always diligent about this.

The tandem sessions are fun, as they are different from taking a class, and I wind up talking about different things with the different people I do the tandems with. I still feel like I make the same simple grammar mistakes, and forget the same vocabulary, over and over, but I'm hoping that some of the practice is helping my conversational skills. As they say here, *piano, piano* — little by little.

Anyway, la signora della scala knew that another woman in the building, Gemma, was looking for a tandem partner to practice her English. So, la signora played "matchmaker" and put us in touch with each other.

Gemma is a retired elementary school teacher who is a very active 78-year-old. She's actually so busy that it was amazing she could slot me into her schedule: she belongs to several local charitable organizations in addition to being an active grandmother who also does yoga once or twice a week, etc., etc. I wish I had half her energy.

She originally wanted to practice her English because she and her husband needed to prepare for upcoming trips to North America, because her husband's job required going to both California and Vancouver. When she knocked on my door and said the *la signora* had suggested I might be interested in doing a tandem, she didn't know that I'd actually lived in both California and Vancouver. We were a perfect match as tandem partners, as it turned out.

Gemma also really likes to go for walks, and in the warmer weather we're able to go for walks during our tandem session. Of course, we always manage to find a cafe to stop at for a quick espresso – we're both sure it helps with the conversational practice. Coffee and conversation – a fine tradition.

When Gemma has time, she also shows me around the countryside. She has a car, so we can drive up into the hills and see the views, including the valleys filled with miles and miles of apple orchards.

I think I may have mentioned that it's the largest apple-producing area in Europe. These valleys become a beautiful white sea of blossoms in springtime.

Gemma and her family also have a house in the mountains, about an hour away from Bolzano up a winding, switch-back road that should have "I survived" T-shirts like the Hana Highway does in Hawaii. Gemma drives this road regularly, I might add — as I said, at 78 she has far more energy that I have now and is always up for an adventure, when she can find the time.

One of the most interesting things from our conversations is talking with her about life in Bolzano and how it's changed over the years. Gemma grew up around here and has lived in our apartment building for a very long time. Her husband was also active in city government for decades, and I believe in his official role he was instrumental in moving that parking lot underground in order to spruce up Piazza Walther, back in the day.

In the past 78 years, Gemma has seen a lot of changes, but probably the story that has stayed with me the longest was the recent history of the Dominican Church and Gemma's connection to it.

———————————————————

The Dominican Church in Bolzano is a block away from our building.

I pass by it every day on my way to Piazza Walther. I had visited the church a couple of times, walking through the austere-looking cloisters, and timing it right to be able to peak into a couple of the tiny chapels — with ornate frescoes — that are only open to the public at certain times of the month. It was all interesting to see, but I didn't learn anything from those visits about the story of the church, or why these days the cloisters are not used as cloisters, or why most of the connected buildings are used now for non-religious purposes.

However, I got a much better idea about the recent history of the church from a visit I made there one day with Gemma last spring, when there was a special exhibit that focused on the history and reconstruction of both the frescos and the church itself following World War II.

It turns out that the cloisters were decommissioned – if that's the right word – back before World War I, and the buildings next to the church were turned into a military hospital for a time. Later, the military used the buildings for other purposes. Later still, during World War II, the church was bombed in the air raids (by the allies) which really were targeting the nearby train station.

Today, the church and at least three of the small chapels have been restored, as well as parts of the old cloister passageways.

The buildings that had been for the nuns and monks are now used for a music conservatory, as well as for an art gallery.

Gemma not only grew up here in Bolzano, but she also attended this church as a child, both before and after the destruction. She was also married in one of the tiny, narrow chapels to the side of the main church, which was mostly destroyed in the bombing as well. There are beautiful frescos in that small chapel that have now been fully restored; she said that during their wedding ceremony in the 1950s, the walls and roof had been resurrected, but the frescoes were still in tatters. I forgot to ask her if the beautiful ceiling that is decorated in blue and covered with stars had also been put back by then.

The Franciscan cloisters, elsewhere in town, are usually where I take visitors if they are here only for a day or two, since they are in some ways more atmospheric and have more frescoes surviving in the passageways. But the Dominican church has a good excuse for only having the structure of the cloisters remaining, with no frescos at all on the surviving walls. When you see the photos of how it was almost completely destroyed in the bombing, it's a wonder they were able to put anything of it back together at all.

When I said to Gemma that it was surprising to me how well they were able to restore the fresco fragments in the chapels and church proper, where the walls were seemingly completely destroyed, she commented that in Italy they are used to having to restore frescos. The damage can come not just from bombing, but also from earthquakes that send walls tumbling down. She pointed out that in Assisi, for example, they have had to repair the paintings in the cathedral there after numerous earthquakes over the years. Reconstructing the walls and frescoes requires painstakingly picking up the pieces of the rubble, large and small, to fit together over a period of years, until the paintings come back to life.

While I knew all these things, somehow talking with someone with a personal connection to a church that was destroyed and has now been completely reconstructed gave a new perspective on the cycle of destruction and rebirth. Although Gemma does speak English well enough to explain these kinds of things, learning her language — and being able to talk with her in it on different topics — has opened up a whole new world to me in terms of understanding life in Bolzano. And that has provided motivation for improving my Italian language skills that you just can't get from a class.

Oops, look at the time. Here I've been rambling on, and it's just about time for Chris to arrive home for lunch. Come back into the kitchen with me while I put the bounty from our morning expeditions to good. I believe I promised to show you how to slice the pretzels to make those delicious speck sandwiches....

Life on a Gelato Diet

So, did you have a good lunch? What did you think of that pretzel and speck sandwich? Good, eh? I never would have thought a pretzel could act as a roll like that, but that mix of salty bread and salty ham is quite tasty.

So, what would you like to do now? Typically at this time of day I take a look at my list and then head out for a few more errands if anything was left undone in the morning. But I think we managed to squeeze everything I'd intended for today in this morning, which is not something I always do.

Plotting my errands according to when places are open here is something I need to consider every day. Most stores open in the morning sometime between 8:00am — 9:30am and stay open until 12:30pm or 1pm, then close for a while, re-opening between 3pm and 4pm. They then stay open until 6:30pm or 7pm. Well, most, but not all stores do that. Despar, that supermarket we visited this morning, is open continuously during the day, as is the downtown branch of the UPIM department store, and a few other shops here and there. But not all of the big chain stores are open continuously. For example, the big electronics store where I bought Chris the razor closes in the middle of the day just like the smaller shops. Also, most stores aren't open much on the weekend, except for Saturday mornings. They are sometimes open on Saturday afternoons — but they are *never* open on Sundays.

This is very different from Verona, an Italian city where Chris and I go often on vacation. Most stores in Verona close in the middle of the day there just like here, but they are also open all day on Saturdays, and sometimes also on Sundays. The Bolzano store hours are also very different from everywhere I've lived as an adult in North America, where stores are open long hours everyday of the week, including Sunday.

Anyway, I'm not sure exactly why, but I had trouble getting used to the schedule here. It's only an issue at times because I still haven't gotten the right mental model for the order in which to do my daily errands if I need to do something that isn't ordinarily part of my routine. So, at least once a week I wind up realizing that I have missed my chance in the morning or early afternoon for some store, and I need to wait until it reopens. It's a good thing I have unlimited time to complete my errands each day, so that I have time to go back out and get whatever I mis-timed in the morning. I'm not sure why I can't get all the different schedules memorized better. Perhaps it's getting used to the fact that while I'm free all the time during the day, the stores aren't.

But in the spring and summer this occasional lack of precise planning works to my advantage, since the afternoon round of errands can be accompanied by a scoop of gelato from one of the numerous speciality shops in town. Perhaps you noticed that small gated storefront across from the bank this morning? That's one of my go-to gelato places in the summer, when the heat and humidity conspire to keep my afternoon walks as brief as possible. That gelato shop isn't the best in town, but it's less than five minutes from our apartment. My favorite shop is over in the Gries part of town, a good 12-minute walk away. I know, it's not *that* much farther. But the difference between a five-minute walk and a 12-minute walk in the sweltering 100 degree Fahrenheit temperatures in July is considerable.

Now, the gelato stores also have special schedules: they aren't open in the mornings, but stay open late in the evenings, and sometimes might even be open on Sundays. But unfortunately, they aren't open at all in the winter: the gelato season is really spring and summer, and maybe early fall. I know, maybe you thought here in Italy people eat gelato all year round. And it is true that you can buy packaged stuff in the supermarket all year round. But real gelato — well, at least really good, made-in-the-store gelato — is a seasonal food. It's been a sign of the changing seasons when the gelato places start to open up in March and April, or start to shut down in September. That Edy coffee bar, where we went for coffee this morning, actually is one of the first to start setting up their gelato freezer at the merest hint of spring weather: it's my signal better weather is just around the corner.

Now, in addition to the supermarket, there are a few bars that also offer ice cream all year round, but those tend to be the places that sell the supermarket-type stuff. I don't recommend them at all. One place on the edge of Piazza Walther sells a mix of fancy sundaes and such all year long aimed at the tourists who will indiscriminately eat big bowls of mediocre gelato when topped with frozen fruit any time of the year. The first year we were here we'd noticed a particular bar like this advertising something called *Eis Spaghetti*, which translates to "spaghetti ice cream." Chris was all set to try it, but the shop's machine to make it was never working whenever we would try to go there.

But then last year we finally found *Eis Spaghetti* down in Trento, the next big town heading south by train from Bolzano. We were walking by a gelato shop when we saw a sign for *Spaghetti Gelato*, which is the Italian version of of the German *Eis-Spaghetti*. It turns out to be a dish with whipped cream on the *bottom* , topped with *spaghetti gelato*, which is a vanilla gelato fed through a machine to give it a "spaghetti strands" shape. That's topped with a strawberry sauce to look like tomato sauce, plus some "grated cheese" made of coconut shavings to top it off. Cute. It tasted like a strawberry ice cream sundae, with an odd sensation of eating through the ice cream and ending with the whipped cream as the final taste. As ice cream sundaes go, it was decent, but it certainly wasn't the best example of gelato we've had in Italy.

And I certainly have tasted a lot of gelato since we've been here. It was so hot that first summer that I embarked on what I started to refer to as my "gelato diet". After all, on a hot and steamy summer day, nothing cools you off like a refreshing scoop of gelato. So, I got in the habit of having a scoop every day as I walked around town, either exploring or doing the daily errands. You might think by doing that I would have tried a lot of different flavors of gelato by now, but in fact, I've had a lot more lemon or *amerena* (sour cherry) flavored gelato than anything else. Those are two flavors that all the places always seem to have, and there's not a lot of time typically for me to peruse the selections on offer before they are asking to take my order. I mean, as soon as I set foot in the store, they think I'm ready to order. I'm guessing that they assume that I knew what I wanted before I ever got there. It's an instance of the same kind of phenomenon that Chris and I have noticed when ordering food at a restaurant, actually. As Chris commented at one point, going to a restaurant in Italy seems to be all about knowing your mind for what you want *before* you ever arrive at the restaurant. I mean, in North America, figuring out what you want to order at a restaurant is typically done after you get there, based on what's listed on the menu, and/or on the the list of the daily specials. Unless you have a favorite dish at a restaurant you patronize regularly, generally you don't go into a restaurant in North America with a specific idea of what you're going to order. OK, well, at least Chris and I don't.

However, based on our unscientific observations in Italy, it would seem that around here, locals go into a restaurant having already figured out what they want to eat, and then, after some discussion with the server, they order that, whether it's on the menu or not. So the menu apparently only serves as a general guide to what ingredients the place has on hand, along with some suggestions on how they *could* prepare those things for you, if you're in the mood for what they've listed. But that's just the starting point for a long discussion about how the dishes are prepared, what other things they could do as variations on a theme with those same ingredients, etc.

Now the by-product of this behavior is that, invariably, the server approaches your table and asks to take your order almost immediately after you've been seated. There's no time to look at the menu before this happens. Similarly, in a place where the specials are read aloud, the server reels off the list for you, and then immediately looks at you, pen poised, ready to write down your order, expecting that you'll order right away. We have come to the conclusion that if most people know what they want to order before they get there, the menu is clearly superfluous, and so the server naturally concludes that you'll be ready to order the moment you sit down.

However, Chris and I are never ready immediately. As a result, we always clearly stand out as foreigners in a restaurant. We usually need and/or want to read the menu and think about the food on offer first, all of which takes us a few minutes. But that's a few minutes longer than anyone else in the restaurant. We wind up having to tell the server to go away and come back, which is so atypical that it can have the unfortunate consequence of our sometimes having to wait quite a while for the server to return. Of course, asking for time to look at the menu is the typical North American procedure, and we find that we haven't quite gotten past that yet. Which is kind of a pity, since it seems like the locals, who know exactly what they want to eat even if it's not offered on the menu, have a completely different idea about what eating out is really all about. We don't quite understand it yet.

However, our needing to browse the menu may be a hard habit for us to shake, even though browsing in general isn't something you ever get to do in most settings here, actually. For example, in a clothing store, a sales person pounces on you as soon as you enter, seeking to find out what you're looking for. If you tell them you're looking for X, the sales person will helpfully start to bring examples of X for you to consider. While such service is very nice sometimes, it doesn't match my typical strategy for clothes shopping, which consists more of browsing the racks to see if there's anything interesting to be had first, and then asking to try it on.

But see, that's not how it works here. You just stepped into a clothing shop? Well, it must be because you needed a specific article of clothing, and not because you just want to have a glance at the merchandise in the store. I went into a shirt-shop once, and there was no casual looking over their stock. It was just a series of questions: long-sleeve or short? red? blue? another color? fancy or plain? etc. etc. And then about 10 shirts came out as a starting point for my consideration.

See, that's why I think that the restaurant ordering behavior here is just an extension of this "no-browsing" general behavior. You just stepped into a restaurant? It must be because you wanted a specific type of food to start with. What's your baseline expectation: do you want a pasta dish? OK. Long or short pasta? Filled or not? Tomato-based sauce or butter and sage? Spicy or not? It's a dialog about the menu possibilities, rather than making you conform to something already on the menu. Very interesting, but we still don't really have the hang of it. But our point and choose "foreigner" method at least usually always gets us something tasty, so I guess ultimately there's nothing really wrong with that.

Now with gelato, it's the advanced level of "knowing your mind" ordering. There's no question and response system — gelato is a frozen cream dessert, where the flavor is the only variable and so they can't really ask about all the flavors, you have to read the signs and figure out the what they happen to have that day. Unlike gelato places in North America — or even some places in Southern Italy — you won't see open bins with the gelato. Instead, all the metal bins containing the gelato are covered, opened only when the clerk is dishing up an order.

So if you know what you want, you can look on the list for it, and it's either there or it isn't. But to someone like me, who doesn't know all the names of all the flavors in Italian, I'm mostly stuck with lemon or amarena, unless there's a line and I have time to study the list and look for another flavor I recognize.

Now one word I recognized on the gelato list one day at my favorite place was "Avocado". The first time I saw it listed, I thought well, maybe "Avocado" was the Italian word for something other than, well, avocado. But no, there was a picture of the ingredient next to the word on the list of flavors, and the picture looked just like an avocado.

It took me a while to work up the nerve to try it, but one day late in the summer I realized I was running out of time to do it before the place closed for the season. But still … I wasn't completely committed to trying something so odd, since they also still listed their mango flavor. Their mango gelato tastes just like a mango — so good, and its one of my standard alternates when it's on the list (which it isn't always). So I wimped out on the avocado decision and went with the sure-thing: mango.

But then the clerk came back and said that they only had enough mango for half a serving, so what did I want for the other half?

Was this a sign? Go for the avocado or the safer lemon choice?

Well, I hedged my bets and asked her how the avocado flavor was. Now, I'm a semi-semi-regular there, in that they recognize me and always greet me like a regular, but we don't chat much beyond that. The same clerk had once suggested I try a taste of their Quark flavor gelato before I committed to a whole scoop of it, so I knew it was possible to get a taste of an unusual gelato flavor in this store. But that's not always the case in Italy. It's actually interesting that, unlike in North America, it isn't common here to ask for a taste of a gelato flavor before you get it. It's not unheard of, but I've noticed hardly anybody does it — as I said, locals know their mind before they set foot in a store or gelato shop.

But since that same clerk had offered me a taste of something in the past, and since they weren't busy at that moment, and well, heck, since we were talking about *avocado* as a gelato flavor, I asked for a taste of it first. As it turned out, It had a creamy avocado flavor with vanilla overtones. Quite tasty. Perhaps vegetables make for good gelato after all — who would have thought, eh?

Now, you might guess that I would have put on a lot of weight as a result of all my gelato sampling. But after eating one scoop of gelato every single day for the first four months we lived in Italy, I wound up shedding many pounds. In fact, since we moved here, I have lost almost 20 pounds, even though properly following a gelato diet is a struggle in the winter, when all the gelato places are closed.

Of course, in addition to eating my scoop-a-day of gelato I am also getting plenty of exercise everyday, what will my morning expeditions and afternoon follow-up excursions, plus other exploring, etc. So you're probably thinking that maybe my weight loss wasn't *really* due to eating all that gelato after all.

But consider the fact that during the winter months my

weight loss actually tapers off, which I think is because I can't eat a scoop of gelato everyday in the winter. Of course, one could argue that I also might be getting less exercise when the weather is cold and rainy. OK, well, maybe I don't go walking around as much in the afternoon, that's true, but my morning routine is pretty much the same, rain or shine, summer or winter.

However, I think the best evidence for the weight-loss power of gelato is my story of our trip to Bologna last year. Now, before Chris and I went to Bologna I'd read stories about four different places that vie for the "Best Gelato in Bologna" and/or the "Best Gelato in Italy" titles. So I felt it was my duty to try these places. I mean, I needed to do research, right? So I made it my goal while I was in Bologna to go to as many gelato places as possible. It's good to have goals.

Now, my "gelato diet" in Bolzano is just one scoop per day, since it's possible to order just one scoop at a time in Bolzano. But elsewhere in Italy, including in Bologna, it's more common for the "small" size servings to be *two* scoops at a time, not just one. Risking the possible effectiveness of my gelato diet, I therefore decided to try *two* scoops servings in Bologna. Which meant that I ordered and ate two scoops of gelato at each place I visited in Bologna.

On the first day, I visited three places. Yes, three gelato shops — all in one day. Ultimately, I had gelato five times over that three day period in Bologna, and each time I had a serving of two scoops. This really helped me meet my research goals. I can tell you with great authority, by the way, that the best place for gelato in Bologna is called _ il Gelatauro_ — they have an outstanding pistachio gelato, a very good chocolate gelato, and a "fennel seed" flavor which was probably *the best* gelato I have ever had. Wow, was that good!

So let's tally up those servings. I had two scoops of gelato on five separate occasions during a three days in Bologna. That's ten scoops of gelato consumed in just *three* days. You might think, then, that afterwards I'd be rethinking the power of a "gelato diet" as a weight loss regimen. After all, in addition to all the gelato I ate there, I also consumed a series of calorie-laden regular meals, mostly pasta with rich meat sauces. When I got home I was a little hesitant to step on the scale, but finally worked up the nerve.

And I discovered that I'd *lost* two pounds. Now, if that's not proof of the effectiveness of gelato for weight loss, what is, eh?

But as I said, during the winter, gelato places are closed. While that means my weight loss regimen gets put on hold, there's still good news when it comes to sweets, as winter is when the cookie season begins!

OK, so I'm joking a little when I call it a "cookie season". But I had a serious craving for a cookie on day in October last year, so I went to buy one at a bakery that I pass every day.

And ... there was nary a cookie in sight. I tried at another bakery that day ... and still no cookies. And again at a third ... no luck. There was a distinct lack of anything resembling a cookie in bakeries in Bolzano in the middle of October. I found that really odd.

But then at the beginning of November, the shelves in the bakeries were suddenly covered in cookies. Cookie season had clearly begun. Now, gelato as a seasonal food I can understand. But cookies have a season, too? Really? Who knew.

Although, I guess it makes a sort of sense, since the first year we were here we had discovered that there's a season for doughnuts (*Krapfen*) in Bolzano, too. If doughnuts can have a season, I guess, why not cookies?

In fact, in January the pastry shops will all be filled with *Krapfen*. It's pretty striking when that happens, since in summer and fall it can be hard to spot any trace of a doughnut. Unlike in North America, *Krapfen* are not for breakfast here, either. Rather, they are considered a dessert pastry for *after* a meal. They come in both regular sizes and mini sizes and are typically filled with jam, although you can also find ones with custard filling, although they aren't as common.

Anyway, the *Krapfen* come out in January and stick around during the Carnival season leading up to Lent. They disappear from the stops on Ash Wednesday, the first day of Lent. They then make a brief re-appearance for Father's Day in Italy in early March, but then they disappear again until the following January. I guess I should have warned you before you came to visit that you should time your trips based on the season for the sweet you crave. Here's a look at the schedule:

November -Easter (March/April): Cookies New Year's Day through Mardi Gras: Doughnuts/*Krapfen* Father's Day in March: Doughnuts/*Krapfen* March/April - October: Gelato

Note that *Krapfen* season overlaps a bit with cookie season, so if you like them both, plan accordingly.

Of course, once gelato season starts, I'll be back to my daily scoop of gelato. Truly, by sticking to the tenets of my "gelato diet," I have lost a lot of weight since I've been in Bolzano and am probably in the best physical shape of my life.

Now, keep in mind that a principle of my gelato diet is typically eating only *one* scoop at a time, and combining that walking everywhere and carrying all my purchases home without a car. Again, the last two are things I do every day, regardless of the availability of gelato. Exercise and otherwise healthy eating therefore admittedly play a big part in my gelato diet, and the gelato itself is not always required. But it is striking to think that I have been consuming regular quantities of gelato since we moved to Bolzano and am now 20 pounds lighter than I'd been on the day we arrived, as I mentioned a moment ago.

Of course, if I take a moment to reflect back to when we first came to Italy, I also realize how much I've changed in so many different ways that have nothing to do with losing weight. It was striking recently to hear friends here describe me as a person they think of as always being calm and patient. That's *not* how people who knew me when I worked in the high-tech industry years ago would have described me, I don't think, where my patience often ran thin under the constant pressures of deadlines and day-to-day chaos.

But in an odd way, my changes in attitude probably do come directly from my adopting this "gelato diet" lifestyle. For instance, I've learned the value of strategic planning, prompted originally by a desire to optimize my route for my errands during those first hot summer months; there was value in making sure I would be walking by my favorite gelato shops at just the right moments when they were open. As a result of the need for pre-planning, I've been forced to become better organized to stay on track to get all my errands done in a timely manner. This has, in turn, made me less frazzled at the end of the day, since I usually manage to accomplish what I set out to do, and therefore overall I'm not worried about getting things done.

I've also gained renewed determination to try things outside my comfort zone, adopting an approach that welcomes the unknown with a bold sense of adventure. For example, if you'd have told me before I moved to Italy that I'd be regularly eating *avocado* gelato, I would have thought you were crazy. Just the idea of it is bizarre enough to have made me think twice before trying it back then. And yet here I am, counting the days until that shop opens up again, so I can get my avocado gelato fix. Branching out in the gelato shops has re-enforced the notion that it's always good to try something once; you never know if that thing you've never dared to try before will become something you actually love.

It's been the same thing with learning to speaking Italian. Before we moved here, I was worried that I'd never be able to open my mouth and speak Italian in public, afraid of making too many grammatical mistakes and looking foolish. I feared it would take years before I'd be comfortable trying. But completing my everyday expeditions in English wasn't ever an option in Bolzano, where hardly anyone speaks English. So it was either plunge in feet first and try to speak a local language or remain isolated at home. Having made the decision to dive in, I discovered that a friendly smile while attempting to communicate really can take you past those awkward moments when you're stumbling around and looking for the right word. As you may have noticed today, I'm now at the point where I really enjoy my daily interactions with all those people I sort-of-know, whose positive encouragement on my limited Italian gives me the motivation to keep learning more.

This gelato diet lifestyle has also reminded me about the importance of reducing the stress in my life. Nothing signals relaxation more than taking the time to buy and eat a scoop of gelato during the day, no matter how many things are on my to-do list. And being able to keep on a even keel day-to-day means I'm not at all stressed out when things go out-of-whack and all those out-of-the-ordinary situations crop up. That things might not go as planned is inevitable, no matter where you live. Rolling with the punches is easier if you can relax, though, and welcome each unexpected experience, unanticipated encounter or even just the next unusual flavor of gelato.

Plus, leading life on a gelato diet gives you a built-in excuse to eat all that wonderful gelato everyday. Life doesn't get much better than that.

Wow, look at the time! It's already past 4pm. There's so much more to show you in Bolzano, but we're clearly not going to have time for it all today. You'll definitely need to come back for another visit. For example, while we did a lot this morning, we didn't do any errands on the other side of the bridge except for the dry cleaners. But several days a week I actually start my errands over there, at the shop where they sell the best fresh fish in town. The friendly women who work there all sort-of-know me and give me tips on the freshest catch of the day, plus advice on how to cook it. Thanks to them, I also now know the trick of quickly deboning and cleaning fresh anchovies, since the women thought I was crazy to pay the extra price to have them do it for me. Have you ever had fresh anchovies? They are nothing like the salted ones you put on pizza, but are light and delicious when quickly pan-fried.

Plus, there's a deli over on that side of the bridge where the owner aspires to have a cafe someday, and he offers a few prepared foods around lunch time on occasion. His dishes are delicious and very unusual for this area, where the concept of prepared foods-to-go is an anomaly.

We haven't made it out to any of the castles around town, nor taken any of the three cable cars up into the mountains, nor explored any of the paintings and passageways in the two old cloisters. So much to experience in this beautiful part of the world, and so little time.

But all that talk about sweets before has given me an idea. Let's head out for a quick jaunt over to the Gries part of town. It's the area where Chris and I stayed when we first arrived here, before we moved into our apartment — only about a 15 minute walk from where we are now. My favorite bakery is over there, too, next to our old hotel in Piazza Gries, and we should be able to find a delicious cookie or two there this time of year. 'Tis *that* season, after all, and the cookies will tide us over until dinner.

Besides, we should seize the chance to try what's available for those treats while we can. After all, even without a scoop of gelato in hand, one learns to make the most of everything around when living life on a gelato diet.

_____

Acknowledgments

I'm extremely grateful to all my friends and family who have provided feedback on my writing encouraged me over the years to put together a book collection of these stories that started their life as a blog.

A special thanks to Dovie, who donated her time and expertise not only to do the final proofreading, but also to make suggestions to improve the final manuscript.

To say that my husband, Chris, has been instrumental in the completion of this work is almost an understatement. Thank you for everything, including — but not limited to! — all the fact-checking, proofreading and technical support at the eleventh hour. Most of all, thank you for giving me the opportunity and inspiration to follow my dream of writing a book about our life in Bolzano.

About the Author

L. Lee McIntyre is an American photographer born in New Jersey, who went from spending summers as a child travelling up and down the Eastern United States to roaming around the world. At last count, she's visited 5 continents, living on 3 of them in 5 different countries. She's also travelled and taken photographs in at least 20 more. Along the way, she worked as a pianist, musical director, freelance journalist, visiting professor of Linguistics, ESL teacher, and software designer before turning to photography full-time.

Lee currently lives in Tuebingen, Germany, where she writes books, takes photos, conducts photography workshops, and gives lectures on the history of American photography, when she's not busy trying to master doing all sorts of everyday expeditions in German without a daily scoop of gelato.

Check Lee's website[1] at clfoto.net for updates on her current projects.

---

[1]http://www.clfoto.net

CPSIA information can be obtained
at www.ICGtesting.com
Printed in the USA
FSHW021001071020
74565FS

9 781497 599635